D0788957

Mismapping the Underworld

Daring and Error in Dante's 'Comedy'

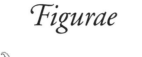

Figurae

READING MEDIEVAL CULTURE

Mismapping the Underworld

Daring and Error in

Dante's 'Comedy'

John Kleiner

Stanford University Press, Stanford, California, 1994

Stanford University Press
Stanford, California
© 1994 by the Board of Trustees of the
Leland Stanford Junior University
Printed in the United States of America

CIP data appear at the end of the book

Stanford University Press publications are
distributed exclusively by Stanford University Press
within the United States, Canada, and Mexico;
they are distributed exclusively by
Cambridge University Press
throughout the rest of the world.

"You know," he continued, shaking Pnin's hand, "I am rereading *Anna Karenin* for the seventh time and I derive as much rapture as I did, not forty, but sixty years ago, when I was a lad of seven. And, every time, one discovers new things—for instance I notice now that Lyov Ni-kolaich does not know on what day his novel starts: it seems to be Friday because that is the day the clockman comes to wind up the clocks in the Oblonski house, but it is also Thursday as mentioned in the conversation at the skating rink between Lyovin and Kitty's mother."

"What on earth does it matter," cried Varvara. "Who on earth wants to know the exact day?"

—Nabokov, *Pnin*

Acknowledgments

Many people have helped in various ways to bring this book into being. John Freccero, Robert Harrison, and Jeffrey Schnapp were my dissertation advisors at Stanford; their guidance and expert skepticism have shaped nearly every chapter that follows. Rachel Jacoff also helped me to discern the early shape of my argument and has continued to offer critical guidance and encouragement. Without her friendship, writing on Dante would have seemed a far stranger and more solitary exercise. Among the other friends and advisors who have along the way made especially important contributions are John Pemberton, Frederick Griffiths, David Halperin, Mary Jean Corbett, Madeleine Kahn, Douglas Biow, Laura Barile, Cassandra Cleghorn, and Shawn Rosenheim. Fellowships from the Mellon Foundation and the Stanford Humanities Center allowed me the free time to pursue this project, and the following journals were kind enough to let me reprint, in new form, earlier articles: *Dante Studies*, *Stanford Italian Review*, and *Texas Studies in Language and Literature*. I am also indebted to Helen Tartar, Sean Keilen, and the staff of the Stanford University Press for their assistance in preparing the manuscript and to the librarians of the rare book collections at Williams College and Stanford University for their good-humored help tracking down early maps of Hell. My final debt is to my wife, editor, and companion in error, Betsy Kolbert.

A Note on the Texts Used

For the Italian text of the *Comedy* I am relying on *The Divine Comedy*, translated with commentary by Charles Singleton, vol. 1, *Inferno*; vol. 2, *Purgatorio*; vol. 3, *Paradiso* (Princeton: Princeton University Press, 1970, 1973, 1975). English translations of the *Comedy* will follow loosely those of Singleton. For the Italian text of the *Vita nuova* I am relying on the *Vita nuova—Rime*, edited by Fredi Chiappelli (Milan: Mursia, 1965). Translations of the *Vita nuova* follow Mark Musa, *Dante's Vita nuova* (Bloomington: Indiana University Press, 1973). For Roman authors I use the Loeb Classical Library editions (Cambridge: Harvard University Press) unless otherwise noted.

Contents

Figures

Mismapping the Underworld

Daring and Error in Dante's 'Comedy'

Introduction

The science of life or of creation is gathered here in its essence and presented with the extreme of clearness and consistency. And by means of the architecture, so coherent and significant in its large lines and so accurate in its smallest details, the intellectual harmony is made into a living thing.[1]

A single man, a solitary man, sets himself face to face with an entire millennium and transforms that historical world. Love, order, salvation are the foci of his inner vision—spheres of light in which immense tensions are collected. They dart together, circle one another, become constellations, figures. . . . From every point of his mythically and prophetically amplified experience connections run to every point of the given matter. They are forged and riveted in material as hard as diamonds. A structure of language and thought is created—comprehensive, with many layers of meaning, and as inalterable as the cosmos.[2]

On reading passages like these, a late-twentieth-century American writing on Dante might well feel a little lonely and impoverished. The essences of creation, the living harmonies, the diamond-hard structures and cosmic patterns that once excited De Sanctis and Curtius are simply no longer accessible. To use such expressions now would be to court from one's readers the charge of mystification. What, they would ask, is "diamond-hard" about a poem? How does a fixed arrangement of words become a "living thing"? Nor is the critic's loss a purely semantic one; the limits imposed on our vocabulary reflect a fundamental change in our vision of poetry and poets. The solitary magician, alchemist, cosmographer-poet has been replaced in our imaginations by a more skeptical, more constrained, and more devious kind of writer—someone who is, on the whole, much more like ourselves.

But if the shifting currents of literary studies have drawn us far from the verdant shores where rhetorical figures once flourished gigantically, we do enjoy as critics some modest advantages. Our current disenchantment has disclosed a set of topics that would have been either inaccessible or unappealing to earlier generations. Perhaps for the first time, it is not only poetry's achievements that seem worth analyzing, but also its limits and illusions. This study clearly reflects this shift in emphasis; rather than exploring Dante's "mythically and prophetically amplified experience," it addresses a miscellaneous assortment of apparently trivial discrepancies—a flawed experiment, a mismeasured giant, an inaccurate translation.

I have chosen to write about such minor imperfections for several reasons: first, because the idea of perfection plays such a central role within Dante's poetry; second, because the study of anomaly is, I think, an effective way to lay bare some of the assumptions that have shaped six centuries of Dante scholarship; and finally, because the errors are fun and, oddly enough, beautiful. If there is a moral to this study, it is that instead of suppressing anomalies, cruxes, and contradictions, we might as well learn to enjoy them.

The three central chapters each treat a different type of crux and the responses it has engendered. In the title chapter, I focus on the efforts made to map Dante's Hell during the Renaissance, and then again at the end of the nineteenth century. This cartographic tradition, I suggest, demonstrates both scholars' fascination with the order of Dante's fiction and their reluctance to take seriously any inconsistencies in it. The next chapter deals primarily with Dante's reputation as an erudite student of classical literature. Focusing on two cantos from the *Inferno* and *Purgatorio*, I discuss the problems presented by Dante's inaccurate citations of Virgil, Statius, and other pagan poets. The fourth chapter moves from literary to scientific error. Here the problems I analyze are not the obvious ones associated with all medieval models of the cosmos, but rather problems that Dante goes to great lengths to invent: what I study are his exacting descriptions of unobservable astronomical events and his design of an experiment that is impossible to perform.

Framing this central sequence are two chapters devoted to analyzing Dante's sense of poetic form. The first chapter takes up numerology and the long-standing debate over whether there is a center to the *Vita nuova*. The final chapter focuses on the encounter with Geryon—the monster who comes at the *Inferno*'s center. These chapters are intended to show how assumptions about the medieval "passion for order" have led critics to underestimate Dante's tolerance, even enthusiasm, for imperfection, asymmetry, and monstrosity.

Readers familiar with the commentary tradition will note that my investigation into the *Comedy*'s anomalies and contradictions is far from comprehensive. Indeed, many of the inconsistencies that historically have attracted the most attention—the conflicting astronomical data of the *Purgatorio*, the divergent accounts of Adamic language provided in the *De vulgari* and *Paradiso*, the puzzling waterways of Hell, and the famous "enigma of the Naiads"—are never directly addressed. Nor can this study be described as a selective but representative survey, because it treats only vexed sections whose difficulties can, I feel, be shown to be deliberately designed. That there are errors in the *Comedy* that are not strategic is hardly to be doubted, and I am convinced, moreover, that a systematic analysis of such unsystematic errors could be extremely rewarding. Yet such a project is for a reader working within a different interpretive framework. Though I realize there are hazards in setting out to discover an author's intentions, this is essentially my goal. I shall be using the study of error as a means of gauging Dante's views on art, his disposition toward his audience, and his ambitions as a poet. Readers bothered by this emphasis on Dante's controlling intelligence should feel free to view it as an enabling fiction, which in part it is.

Chapter I

Finding the Center

In 1836, in a private letter to a sympathetic friend, Gabriele Rossetti reported a remarkable discovery he had made while studying the *Vita nuova*. This early work of Dante's was, he realized, much more highly structured than any reader had hitherto noticed. If one stripped away the *Vita nuova*'s prose and paid close attention to the arrangement of the remaining lyric poems, one could see that the work possessed a hidden symmetry: the three major canzoni in the collection divide the shorter poems into four evenly balanced groups. The organization of the collection is not random or casual; it is, rather, mathematically exacting:[1]

Ten Minor Poems
Canzone
Four Sonnets
—Central Canzone—
Four Sonnets
Canzone
Ten Minor Poems.

A discovery like Rossetti's invites many different responses. To readers who view secrecy as a writerly virtue, the central pattern might well appear to be evidence of a brilliantly executed reticence: in the *Vita nuova*, Dante strives for and achieves a poetic architecture so subtle that it defeats detection by nearly all his readers. This elusiveness, they might suggest, matches the methods of erotic concealment the lover practices in the pursuit of his beloved—it is the formal equivalent of Dante's outwardly disguised yet inwardly unwavering passion for Beatrice. Other readers, more engaged by notions of poetic control than by secrecy, might choose to focus on the way the Rossettian schema imposes order on an apparently unruly gathering. For such readers, the pattern demonstrates Dante's persistent interest in symmetry. It is, they might suggest, a foretaste of the grander, more complex numerological schemes built into the *Comedy*. For still other readers whose tastes run toward allegoresis, the pattern offers a different kind of promise: here, in the arrangement of the poems, is a key to unlocking the work's meaning. By establishing a center for the work—the canzone "Donna pietosa"—Dante determines the proper course of our interpretive trajectory.

To my mind, these are all promising responses. Whether we choose to focus on the pattern's subtlety, its orderliness, or its message, Rossetti's discovery helps us to appreciate the wonderful strangeness of Dante's enterprise. And yet there are many readers who have staunchly refused to interest themselves in the Rossettian schema. From as early as the turn of the century, critics have repeatedly sought to warn readers against it.[2] These skeptics have denied that the pattern is important, questioned its deliberateness, and cast doubt on the perspicacity of its interpreters. They have argued that the symmetry of the *Vita nuova* is not Dante's creation, but the work of unselfcritical critics: it is, they have claimed, little more than a numerologist's fantasy.

This chapter is about this debate and will present what is, I hope, an objective analysis of the competing arguments. My purpose is not, however, to settle the matter in favor of one side or the other; I am less interested in arguing for a final secure reading of the Rossettian pattern than in using it to plot readerly motives and assumptions. The debate over the *Vita nuova*'s hidden symmetry reveals, I shall suggest, the difficulty

of interpreting patterns that promise more than they achieve—
patterns that seem as if they should be perfectly executed but
are not.

~~~~~~

Of the many scholars to endorse the Rossettian schema, none
has been more eloquent or influential than Charles Singleton.
His *Essay on the "Vita nuova"* has long been recognized as a wa-
tershed in the history of Dante studies, and it is in the pages of
this work that the typical American reader is likely to have first
learned of the *Vita nuova*'s symmetric structure. Though Sin-
gleton's aims are distinctive, his *Essay* nonetheless provides a
useful model for seeing what can be made of a pattern. His
claims about the Rossettian pattern's importance are greater in
scope than those of any critic except, perhaps, Rossetti him-
self.

At the heart of Singleton's *Essay* is a theological theory of
poetic form. Based on citations from Bonaventure, Augus-
tine, and Aquinas, Singleton argues that during the Middle
Ages the art of poetry was understood as an extension of di-
vine art. It was generally accepted, he claims, that "poems ought
to resemble the creation" and that "poets ought to be like God."[3]
In Dante's case, this imitative impulse manifests itself in two
types of analogy: Dante writes poetry that he hopes will reflect
the formal order of the cosmos and the hermeneutic order of
sacred scripture.

Both types of analogy help to explain, and are in turn con-
firmed by, the *Vita nuova*'s hidden pattern. Since symmetry is
a prominent feature of medieval cosmology, it is logical that a
theomimetic poet should wish to order his poems symmetri-
cally.

At a time when this universe of ours revealed to the contemplative
eye of man an order and a harmony expressing the substantial order
and harmony of its Creator, it cannot be insignificant that the micro-
cosmic vision of the poet should reveal a symmetry resembling that
of the greater artifact, the cosmos. Our human art is grandchild to

God's. Being this, it can reflect that light by which all that is intelligible comes from him. (Singleton, p. 7)

Symmetry also functions as a hermeneutic principle because of the peculiar structure of Christian history. In the Christian library, there are essentially two kinds of text corresponding to two distinct historical periods: there is the prospective text of the Old Testament and the retrospective of the New. At the dividing line stands the single critical event—the Crucifixion—to which all biblical narratives are supposed to refer. If a poet is to imitate this structure, then he should locate at the center of his work an event of comparable importance—an event that grants his narrative meaning and direction.[4] In Singleton's account of the *Vita nuova*, this "central" event is Beatrice's death as recorded in the central canzone, "Donna pietosa."

Even as (in the medieval view) the death of our Lord Jesus Christ stands at the center of the whole Christian universe, saying what now is and what then is; and even as all things that come before His death look forward to it and all things that come after His death look back upon it: just so is the death of Beatrice in that little world of the *Vita Nuova* where Beatrice is, as Christ in the real world whose author is God. (Singleton, p. 24)

Viewed through Singleton's eyes, the Rossettian schema is much more than an elegant decoration designed to flatter the knowing eye. Whatever pleasure Dante may have taken in perfecting his pattern is held to be less significant than his ethical responsibility to strive after order and harmony. The work's highly controlled form is treated as if it were a sign of the poet's high moral seriousness. This reading of the *Vita nuova* is powerfully predictive. For if the *Vita nuova* reflects a theological pressure toward symmetry, then that same pressure should be apparent whenever and wherever Dante exercises his creative faculty. Form, in Singleton's account, does not merely express a particular artist's sensibility at a particular moment in his career; it expresses a worldview shared by an entire community.

The prediction implicit in Singleton's reading of the *Vita nuova* has, in fact, been tested with remarkable success. Since the *Essay*'s publication, scholars have discovered dozens of numerical patterns and symmetries unsuspected by previous generations of readers. These range from relatively accessible insights—the realization that like-numbered cantos of the *Inferno*, *Purgatorio*, and *Paradiso* have important thematic ties— to truly abstruse discoveries about the positions of critical words or rhymes.[5] Singleton himself is responsible for bringing to light one of the subtlest of these structures. In 1965 he realized that by counting the number of lines contained in different cantos of the *Purgatorio*, one could reveal a symmetrical pattern centered on the *Purgatorio*'s central canto.[6]

Canto	14	15	16	17	18	19	20
No. of lines	151	145	145	139	145	145	151

One may or may not be attracted to this kind of canto-counting, but one can hardly doubt that Singleton and his followers are responding to something real. They have shown that the *Comedy* exhibits patterns and symmetries that are strikingly inventive and subtle, and that demanded immense labor for their realization. It is clear from their research that structure plays a role in Dante's work far beyond that to which modern readers are accustomed.

But if the *Essay* has pushed critics to make significant discoveries and to rethink their assumptions, the numerological arguments proposed in it are nonetheless seriously flawed, and it is these flaws that I now wish to consider.

꙳

As I noted earlier, the Rossettian schema depends on division of the *Vita nuova*'s lyrics into two basic groups: major canzoni on the one hand, sonnets and other "minor" poems on the other. Once we accept this division, demonstrating the pattern's deliberateness is relatively simple. Let us assume, for the moment, that the *Vita nuova* contains 28 poems of one type

(26 sonnets and 2 non-canzoni) and 3 poems of another (3 canzoni). How likely is it that these 31 poems should fall purely by chance into a symmetrical arrangement? A moment's thought shows that there are fifteen possible symmetrical arrangements: one canzone must go in the middle of the collection and the other two canzoni must go in one of fifteen paired positions on either side. The number of random asymmetrical arrangements is clearly much greater. In fact, the total number of ways of ordering the poems approaches 4,500:

$$N_{total} = \frac{31!}{(28!)(3!)} = \frac{(31)(30)(29)}{(3)(2)(1)} = 4,495.$$

Symmetry could conceivably emerge without any prodding from the poet, but such a felicitous accident is extremely unlikely—the odds against it are roughly 300 to 1.

This clear and simple calculation would settle the matter were it not for a problem glossed over in the preceding paragraph: The calculation depends on assigning each poem to one of two groups, yet several of the poems resist such simple classification. The most problematic poems are the collection's three lyric fragments: the unfinished canzoni of chapters 27 and 33 and the sonnet fragment of chapter 34. In order to reveal (or impose) a symmetric pattern, one must handle these fragments very delicately: the unfinished canzone of fourteen lines must be labeled a sonnet; the unfinished canzone in two stanzas must be labeled a non-canzone; and the brief sonnet fragment must be ignored altogether.[7]

The lyric fragments defy simple classification, and their fragmentary condition itself casts doubt on Singleton's approach. One of the principal contentions of the *Essay* is that medieval poets in general, and Dante in particular, felt a theological compulsion to present finished works. According to Singleton, the completeness of a poem is a sign that it is "designed to reflect God's work in *its* completeness and perfection."[8] If this is the case, then why does Dante admit lyric fragments into the collection? And why does he place them so near the work's end? Reading through the *Vita nuova*, one increasingly confronts poems that seem *im*perfect and *in*complete. The climactic confrontation occurs in the final chapter, where Dante alludes to a "mirabile visione" that he hopes one day to describe—if he lives long enough.

Appresso questo sonetto apparve a me una mirabile visione, ne la quale io vidi cose che mi fecero proporre di non dire più di questa benedetta infino a tanto che io potesse più degnamente trattare di lei. E di venire a ciò io studio quanto posso, sì com'ella sae veracemente. Sì che, se piacere sarà di colui a cui tutte le cose vivono, che la mia vita duri per alquanti anni, io spero di dicer di lei quello che mai non fue detto d'alcuna. (*V.N.* 42.1–2)

After I had written this sonnet there came to me a miraculous vision in which I saw things that made me resolve to say no more about this blessed one until I would be capable of writing about her in a nobler way. To achieve this I am striving as hard as I can, and this she truly knows. Accordingly, if it be the pleasure of Him by whom all things live that my life continue for a few more years, I hope to write of her that which has never been written of any other woman.

This promise of greater things to come, this resolution to remain silent until new skills are achieved, turns the *Vita nuova* into a provisional project—a work whose true end lies in the future. As Robert Harrison observes, "A dramatic failure, an avowed authorial inadequacy, haunt the end of this work."[9]

Another aspect of the *Vita nuova* that Singleton's analysis fails to address is the eccentric placement of Beatrice's death. In the *Essay*, Singleton claims that there is an analogy between Beatrice's death and Christ's: Christ dies and is resurrected at the center of time, Beatrice dies in the canzone that comes at the *Vita nuova*'s center—the canzone "Donna pietosa."

The attentive reader will come to see that the death of Beatrice holds a central position in the *Vita Nuova*. This is true even in point of outward arrangement of the poems. For there are three longer poems so spaced as to mark off the work into three equal parts, and it is the second of these longer poems, the middle one, which gives us Beatrice dead. We see her dead body. Women are covering her face with a veil. (Singleton, p. 7)

Singleton urges the attentive reader to note that Beatrice's death holds a "central position," yet this is not actually the case. The central canzone "Donna pietosa" does not describe Beatrice's real death, but only Dante's vision of her death; the real event comes five chapters and four poems later. The "attentive reader" should recognize the importance of this sleight of hand. By eliding the difference between vision and reality, Singleton deftly avoids having to answer a difficult question: If the center is as important as he claims, then why *doesn't* Beatrice die there? Why should a prophetic dream occupy the formal center of the work instead of the crucial event foreshadowed in that dream?

Singleton speaks enthusiastically of closure and symmetry and invites his readers to admire the medieval artist's devotion to perfectly executed patterns. Yet when it comes to his own theory, he proves something less than a perfectionist. The gaps in his account are so pervasive that he must surely have noticed them and decided to suppress them. In composing the *Essay*, he appears to have realized that the erring details were less important than his larger message, that his theory was too elegant to be sacrificed on account of a few irritating glitches. It is easy to smile at Singleton's compromise with error, but hard to articulate a position that would not be equally inconsistent. Assume, for the moment, that one decides to reject Singleton's reading based on the anomalies and contradictions discussed above. Though such a decision might explicitly release the poet and reader from the charge of obsessive perfectionism, it implicitly reaffirms the perfectionist impulse. To reject the Rossettian schema as imperfectly realized and *therefore* unintended is to assume, with Singleton, that authorial intent and formal perfection are coincident, that the only deliberate patterns are those executed without blemish.

In the remainder of this chapter, I shall pursue a different approach to the *Vita nuova*, partly to bring into focus certain neglected aspects of the work and partly to demonstrate a general analytic method. I propose to show that it is possible to generate an appealing, even genuinely informative reading of the *Vita nuova* in which order and disorder are viewed as complementary rather than opposing categories.

Consider, first, the question of closure. Is the *Vita nuova* a finished or a provisional project? Is Dante striving after perfect symmetry and failing, or is he merely uninterested in it? Nowhere does this question seem more pressing than in the chapters devoted to recording Beatrice's death. At the start of chapter 27, Dante announces that he wants to write a new poem dealing with a new and grander theme: Beatrice's effect on himself. It is a theme that will require, he claims, a full canzone.

E però propuosi di dire parole, ne le quali io dicesse come me parea essere disposto a la sua operazione, e come operava in me la sua vertude; e non credendo potere ciò narrare in brevitade di sonetto, cominciai allora una canzone, la quale comincia: *Sì lungiamente.*

> Sì lungiamente m'ha tenuto Amore
> e costumato a la sua segnoria,
> che sì com'elli m'era forte in pria,
> così mi sta soave ora nel core.
> Però quando mi tolle sì 'l valore,
> che li spiriti par che fuggan via,
> allor sente la frale anima mia
> tanta dolcezza, che 'l viso ne smore.
>
> Poi prende Amore in me tanta vertute,
> che fa li miei spiriti gir parlando,
> ed escon for chiamando
> la donna mia, per darmi più salute.
> Questa m'avvene ovunque ella mi vede,
> e sì è cosa umil, che nol si crede.

XXVIII

Quomodo sedet sola civitas plena populo! facta est quasi vidua domina gentium. Io era nel proponimento ancora di questa canzone, e compiuta n'avea questa soprascritta stanza, quando lo segnore de la giustizia chiamoe questa gentilissima a gloriare. (*V.N.*27–28)

And so I decided to write a poem telling how I seemed to be disposed to her influence, and how her miraculous power worked in me; and believing I would not be able to describe this within the limits of the sonnet, I immediately started to write a canzone which begins: *So long a time.*

> So long a time has Love kept me a slave
> and in his lordship fully seasoned me,
> that even though at first I found him harsh,
> now tender is his power in my heart.
> But when he takes my strength away from me
> so that my spirits seem to wander off,
> my fainting soul is overcome with sweetness,
> and the color of my face begins to fade.

> Then Love starts working in me with such power
> he turns my spirits into ranting beggars,
> and, rushing out, they call
> upon my lady, pleading in vain for kindness.
> This happens every time she looks at me,
> yet she herself is kind beyond belief.

XXVIII

How doth the city sit solitary that was full of people! How is she become a widow, she that was great among nations! I was still engaged in composing this canzone, in fact I had completed only the stanza written above, when the God of Justice called this most gracious one to glory.

For a moment, at least, we are disoriented. Dante has promised to write a full canzone, yet after he has completed only a single stanza, he suddenly starts a new chapter and shifts abruptly from Italian to Latin. Only when we read beyond the quotation from Jeremiah and learn of Beatrice's death can we make sense of what has happened: Beatrice has died while

Dante was in the middle of composing "Sì lungiamente," and that tragedy has permanently deferred the canzone's completion. With Beatrice no longer among the living, the poem's original message and phrasing cease to be appropriate. The fragmentary canzone survives as the visible trace of a crisis that has forced a fundamental change in Dante's art and, one supposes, his life.

If this deployment of a lyric fragment to signal a literary and spiritual crisis is deliberate, as I believe it is, then it expresses an approach to poetic form far more sophisticated than that allowed either by Singleton or by most of Singleton's critics.[10] Fully aware that his readers will associate artistic control with formal closure, Dante deliberately introduces a confusion-producing fragment into his collection. We cannot say that the young poet is either an adept or an opponent of closed literary systems because his performance brings the categories of perfection and imperfection into a creative, meaning-engendering opposition. It is precisely the deferral of the finished lyric that communicates its author's suffering. So artful is this staging of defeat, in fact, that it raises new problems for the readers of the *Vita nuova*. To recognize the significance of the poet's failure is to recognize that his failure is strategic and thus not really a failure at all. Even as Dante announces his terrible incapacitating crisis, he demonstrates a coolheaded virtuosity in manipulating literary conventions.

The ambiguous nature of Dante's artistic failure extends even to the placement of the canzone's fracture. As we noted earlier, the unfinished canzone lasts exactly fourteen lines before being abandoned. It is thus a fragmentary *canzone* that looks uncannily like a perfect *sonnet*. In fact, it exhibits not only the right number of lines, but also essentially the right structure: its *diesis* occurs after the eighth line, and it scans and rhymes much like Dante's other sonnets.[11] Of the 21 canzoni that Dante composed during his life, "Sì lungiamente" is the only one that could suffer such a felicitous incompletion. We could, of course, claim that this is merely an accident, but if this is so, Dante goes to a surprising length to attract our attention to it. Before beginning "Sì lungiamente," Dante explicitly tells us *not* to expect that his next poem will be a sonnet. He cannot write a sonnet because the sonnet would be inadequate to his new theme ("e non credendo potere ciò narrare in brevitade di sonetto, cominciai allora una canzone"). And then, curiously enough, he delivers his sonnet look-alike.

The local shift from canzone to sonnet necessarily affects the larger work's structure. As the *Vita nuova*'s nineteenth poem, "Sì lungiamente" falls in the second group of four sonnets. Thus if it had been completed, we would need to redraw the Rossettian schema as follows:

Ten Minor Poems
Canzone
Four Sonnets
Central Canzone
Three Sonnets
Canzone
Canzone
Ten Minor Poems

This hypothetical arrangement of lyrics is clearly not symmetric. The canzoni and sonnets no longer balance one another, and the collection is no longer centered on the revelatory canzone "Donna pietosa." Had Dante managed to finish "Sì lungiamente," the collection as a whole would have lost its order and its center; Dante only finishes the total work by leaving part of it unfinished.

There are at least two ways to construe Dante's complex use of fragments in the *Vita nuova*. One could claim that in this first extended work, the young poet stages the victory of order over chaos, that he allows a larger, more complete structure to be born from what appears to be a local failure. Or one could claim that the elegant order of the *Vita nuova* masks a fundamental imperfection, that Dante leaves his work, at its very center, unstable and unfinished. It is up to us to choose, but whichever path we follow we should acknowledge the dynamic interdependence of order and disorder, perfection and imperfection.

Let us now turn to the problem of Beatrice's two deaths—one in dream and one in reality. Is there evidence that this awkward doubling is also subject to poetic control, to an art of controlling chaos? To explore this possibility let us broaden the scope of our investigation: instead of worrying solely about the arrangement and articulation of the poems, let us also consider the structure of the *Vita nuova*'s prose.[12]

The prose of the *Vita nuova* fulfills a dual function: it propels forward the narrative of Dante's "new life" while simultaneously providing a running commentary on the poems written in the course of that "new life." As both storyteller and autoexegete, Dante is extremely consistent. To gloss his poems, he always follows the same basic procedure—he divides them into smaller and smaller semantic units that he calls "divisions" (*divisioni*). This process of dividing poems is, Dante claims, a form of revelation: "La divisione non si fa se non per *aprire la sentenzia* de la cosa divisa" (14.13; emphasis mine). Similarly repetitive is Dante's use of chapter headings. Rather than experimenting with different openings as he does in the *Comedy*, Dante builds a narrative frame based on a monotonous sequence of "then, then, then, and then." *Appresso* and *poi* are the first words in half of the *Vita nuova*'s 42 chapters.

The insistent, even wearying uniformity of the prose chapters gives prominence to even the subtlest variations in format. Thus when Dante decides in Chapter 31 to reverse the positions of the poems and the *divisioni*, we immediately sense the change in rhythm; we have moved, it seems, from one section of the work to another. We are similarly affected by the subtle shift in the use of chapter headings: in the austere prose of the *Vita nuova*, we cannot help but notice that Dante begins by favoring *appresso* and then shifts to *poi*. I have cited these specific changes because they are both triggered by Beatrice's death. As Figure 1 indicates, the shift from *appresso* to *poi* and

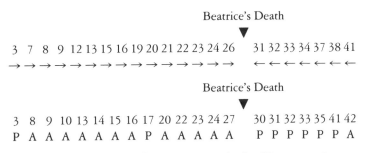

Figure 1. The structure of prose chapters in the *Vita nuova*. Arrows pointing to the right indicate chapters in which the *divisioni* follow the poems; arrows pointing to the left indicate chapters in which the *divisioni* precede the poems. The letter *A* indicates chapters headed by *appresso*; the letter *P* indicates chapters headed by *poi*.

the transposition of the *divisioni* mark Beatrice's death as a formal turning point.

Dante explicitly comments on one of these shifts. In chapter 31, he tells us that he is reversing the order of the poems and the explanatory "divisions" so that the poems following Beatrice's death will seem "more widowed":

E acciò che questa canzone paia rimanere più vedova dopo lo suo fine, la dividerò prima che io la scriva; e cotale modo terrò da qui innanzi. (*V.N.* 31.2)

And in order that this canzone may seem to remain all the more widowed after it has come to an end, I shall divide it before I copy it. And from now on I shall follow this method.

Though the precise meaning of this metaphor is by no means obvious, I think we can safely infer a connection between mourning and memory. When Dante speaks of a poem as being "widowed," he is suggesting that its orientation is essentially retrospective and memorial. This is true of all the poems following Beatrice's death insofar as they come after the "central" event of Dante's new life; every poem after chapter 31 takes its meaning from the past. The transposition of poem and gloss can also be said to represent a form of "widowing" because it establishes a new temporality of reading: in the new order, readers do not *look forward* to the gloss that will explicate the poem; instead, they are called upon to *remember* the gloss that they have already read.

Given Dante's willingness to interpret the positions of poems and divisions metaphorically, it seems likely that the coincident shift from *appresso* to *poi* might also be significant. Though the two terms are close in meaning, they are not identical: *appresso* has a wider, more complex range of associations. When used as an adverb, *appresso* suggests separation, but when used as a preposition, it suggests proximity and is closely related to the verb *appressare*. These conflicting senses of *appresso* mirror the complex relations between events occurring before Beatrice's death. In this period of Dante's life, events follow *after* one another but also point *toward* the event that will determine their meaning. *Appresso* ceases to be the proper conjunction between different chapters as soon as Beatrice's death occurs; from that point onward, the poet no longer progresses toward the future, but simply moves away from the past. The only post-Beatrice appearance of *appresso* as a chapter heading occurs, appropriately enough, in the final chapter when Dante looks *forward* to his future work.

Appresso questo sonetto apparve a me una mirabile visione, ne la quale io vidi cose che mi fecero proporre di non dire più di questa benedetta infino a tanto che io potesse più degnamente trattare di lei. (*V.N.* 42.1–2)

After I had written this sonnet there came to me a miraculous vision in which I saw things that made me resolve to say no more about this blessed one until I would be capable of writing about her in a nobler way.

The signposts that mark the center of the prose narrative are certainly not obvious, and yet they are not any more obscure than the hidden numerical pattern discovered by Rossetti. If we can believe that one pattern is Dante's deliberate creation, then we might as well believe that the other is as well. The only problem is that the two patterns locate two *different* centers for the work. While the lyric center is Beatrice's visionary death, the prose center is Beatrice's actual death. From a strict Singletonian perspective, such a contradiction is very difficult to explain.[13] For if Dante is trying to imitate God's work, he should not be uncertain about his work's interpretive center. A work that has two centers is potentially unstable, ambiguous, and confusing. In such a work one does not know exactly where to look for the critical signs that will anchor its meaning.

This is an especially serious problem in the *Vita nuova* because the two centers are so different. The dream scene, as Singleton observes, is cast in the readily identifiable form of a revelation. We recognize Dante's crisis not only from his tear-stained face, but also from the heavens themselves. Borrowing the imagery of Revelation 6:12–14, Dante depicts the features of a mourning cosmos:

> E pareami vedere lo sole oscurare, sì che le stelle si mostravano di colore ch'elle mi faceano giudicare che piangessero; e pareami che li uccelli volando per l'aria cadessero morti, e che fossero grandissimi terremuoti. E maravigliandomi in cotale fantasia, e paventando assai, imaginai alcuno amico che mi venisse a dire: "Or non sai? la tua mirabile donna è partita di questo secolo." (*V.N.* 23.5–6)

> And I seemed to see the sun grow dark, giving the stars a color that would have made me swear that they were weeping. And it seemed to me that the birds flying through the air fell to earth dead, and there were violent earthquakes. Bewildered as I dreamed, and terrified, I imagined that a friend of mine came to tell me: "Then you don't know? Your miraculous lady has departed from this world."

Beatrice's actual death, by contrast, is handled with extreme reticence. Dante refuses to speak directly about the most important event in his new life on the apparently paradoxical ground that such a description would be inconsistent with his original plan for the *Vita nuova*. At the very climax of the poet's "new life," Beatrice vanishes into a fold of the narrative he categorically refuses to open.

E avvegna che forse piacerebbe a presente trattare alquanto de la sua partita da noi, non è lo mio intendimento di trattarne qui per tre ragioni: la prima è che ciò non è del presente proposito, se volemo guardare nel proemia che precede questo libello. (*V.N.* 28.2)

And even though the reader might expect me to say something now about her departure from us, it is not my intention to do so here for three reasons. The first is that such a discussion does not fit into the plan of this little book, if we consider the preface which precedes it.

Though the existence of these two competing centers represents a serious problem for Singleton's theory, it is easily accommodated in an interpretive framework that admits tension and fragmentation as valid analytic categories. If there are two centers in the *Vita nuova*—one reticent and one revelatory—then one might venture that that contradiction is itself revealing. It is certainly the case that Dante presents his relation to Beatrice in contradictory ways. Although he repeatedly invokes Beatrice as the figure whose presence authenticates his work, the figure who both inspires his poetry and serves as its subject, he also repeatedly affirms his inability to write a poem adequate to her. This posture toward the beloved is, of course, not unique to Dante, but it has seldom been maintained so resolutely. Every suggestion of Beatrice's animating presence is matched by a complementary suggestion that it is her absence that in fact animates the *Vita nuova*'s poetry. We are regularly reminded that Beatrice's power lies as much in her unbroken silence as it does in her wondrous greeting. And while the poet may never claim to fully appropriate Beatrice, he also never completely renounces his hope of finding adequate words.[14]

As the structural tensions in the *Vita nuova* help us to notice the writer's conflicted desires, so the reverse is also true: acknowledging the rift in Dante's motivations helps us to make sense of his failure to create a perfectly ordered, perfectly coherent work. Ambivalent about his project and "uncentered" as artist, he designs a work with two competing centers, a work pointing simultaneously toward reticence and revelation. In such a reading of the *Vita nuova*, Love's criticism of the "uncentered" lover applies equally well to the artist and to his artifact:

Ego tanquam centrum circuli, cui simili modo se habent circumferentie partes; tu autem non sic. (*V.N.* 12.4)

I am like the center of a circle, equidistant from all points on the circumference; you, however, are not.

The interpretation of the *Vita nuova* that I have just proposed bears obvious similarities to Singleton's. As Singleton plotted the work's structure to disclose its coherence, so have I used its structure to disclose tensions and contradictions. The form of this repetition may, I realize, trouble some readers. While Singleton can claim that the *Vita nuova*'s perfect symmetry reflects a "passion for order" demonstrated by countless medieval artifacts, my approach may appear to present the work as strange and anomalous—an oddly modern-looking experiment in dissonance. Subsequent chapters will, I hope, lessen the appearance of anachronism; one goal of this study is to clarify the roles played by error and disorder within medieval cosmology, hermeneutics, and aesthetics. An even more immediate goal is to describe disorder's role within the *Comedy*. In that later poem, the patterns are clearer and stronger than in the *Vita nuova*; there we find more complex symmetries, more numerical wizardry, and a more insistent emphasis on closure. But that work also reveals the poet's deepening interest in the perils of pretending to perfection and his widening awareness of the gap between human and divine art. On the question of poetic control, the *Comedy* is, I believe, even more ambitiously ambivalent than Dante's first youthful experiment.

Chapter 2

Mismapping the Underworld

The diagrams of Hell that so often accompany new editions of the *Inferno* are a good example of how seriously contemporary critics take Dante's fiction. Each neat picture of carefully layered concentric circles implies that Hell can and should be visualized; each picture reflects a widely held conviction that Hell is an extremely orderly place designed by an extremely exacting poet. Yet in one respect, at least, even the most detailed illustrations are obscure. The diagrams that editors like Singleton, Sayers, and Salinari provide do not indicate precise distances; they do not measure the widths of the circles crossed by Dante in his descent, nor the depths of the pits that he scales.[1] Modern editors may be willing to sketch the general shape of Hell, but they are unwilling to map it in miles and meters.

Earlier generations of scholars were not nearly so hesitant. Until fairly recently, editions of the *Inferno* were routinely accompanied by exacting studies of the terrain and by maps depicting the size of its slopes and circles. Though scholars disagreed (sometimes violently) about the dimensions of specific landmarks, the consensus was that infernal cartography was a legitimate, if difficult, science. This chapter traces the history of infernal cartography from the height of its popularity in the Renaissance to its recent fall into disfavor. I shall ask why mapping the underworld might once have had an enormous appeal to scholars and general readers alike, and why it should now be cast as a bizarre and extravagant enterprise. In the process, I shall try to clear a space for a new reading of the landscape, a reading that focuses on the ambiguous, even deceptive nature of the terrain's description. The final question that I shall ask is not why critics might have produced misleading maps of Dante's underworld, but why Dante might have done so himself.

~~~~

Although discussions, illustrations, and calculations of the infernal terrain are to be found in several trecento manuscripts and commentaries, the heyday of infernal cartography extends from about 1450 to 1600.[2] It is during this period that the shape of Hell emerged as a central critical concern and that numerous scholars set out to measure and debate its dimensions. Two of the first to undertake the project were the Florentine architects Antonio Manetti and Filippo Brunelleschi. No record survives of Brunelleschi's computations, but we know of his interest in the problem from Vasari's *Vite*.[3] Vasari reports that the famous architect studied the proportions of Dante's Hell quite thoroughly, and that when wandering the city and conversing with friends he frequently referred to them. Manetti also enjoyed talking about his work, and his conversations were recorded in much greater detail. In 1481, Landino incorporated Manetti's calculations into his commentary on the *Inferno*; then in 1506, Girolamo Benivieni published a lively dialogue between himself and Manetti in which Manetti's ideas were thoroughly considered.[4]

Both works had a lasting impact on the history of infernal cartography. The Landino commentary was highly respected and widely disseminated. It was reprinted at least a dozen times and attached to most of these editions was Manetti's plan.[5] The cartographic section—a description of the "site, form, and measurements of Hell and the stature of the giants and Satan"—was, moreover, prominently situated as the leading entry in the commentary. Benivieni's treatise was less widely available to Renaissance readers, but it provided a much fuller discussion of Manetti's method and supplied the first drawings of Hell to qualify unambiguously as maps (see Figure 2).[6] On the far right side of the engraving, the artist has indicated the depths of the various circles, and on the left side he has indicated their widths. Limbo, we learn, is $405^{15}/_{22}$ miles beneath the surface of the earth and $87^{1}/_{2}$ miles in width; the circle of the *luxuriosi* is $405^{15}/_{22}$ miles beneath Limbo and 75 miles across. Perhaps inspired by Benivieni, fifteenth-century editors frequently commissioned maps for new editions of the *Inferno*. Maps are included, for example, in the pirated Aldine editions published in 1515 and 1520 (see Figure 3).[7]

Benivieni and Landino both claimed Manetti as the source for their studies, but in 1544, Alessandro Vellutello, a Sienese scholar, set himself up as an independent authority. Based on his close reading of the *Inferno*, he claimed that Manetti and his Florentine followers had overestimated the total size of Hell and had mismeasured several prominent landmarks.[8] Like Landino before him, Vellutello gives his topographic speculations pride of placement, situating them at the very start of his commentary. This topographic section is accompanied by ten elegant engravings—one to illustrate each of Hell's ten circles. At the bottom of each figure, the circle's diameter and depth are measured in miles (see Figure 4).

Vellutello's polemical new map of Hell drew into the debate its most celebrated participant: Galileo Galilei. Galileo's work as infernal cartographer survives (somewhat to the embarrassment of Galileo scholars) in a pair of lectures delivered to the Accademia Fiorentina in 1588.[9] These lectures provide the most striking evidence of infernal cartography's claims to legitimacy among Renaissance readers; nowhere in these lectures does the young mathematician portray infernal mapmaking as misguided or unscientific. On the contrary, Galileo makes a point of putting his scientific training to use whenever possible. He begins his study by citing Archimedes' works on solid geometry to fix the location of the entrance to the underworld. Later, he calculates the strength of stone vaults and estimates the depth of the sea to determine how much earth must be allocated for the roof of Hell to prevent its collapse. Computations like these allow Galileo to announce to his audience that Manetti's map of the underworld is far and away the most accurate and that the Florentine architect has "miraculously" read Dante's mind.[10]

From this brief survey, which neglects some of the Renaissance's minor cartographers, it should be clear that infernal cartography enjoyed, at its peak, a wide and talented audience. How are we to understand such a curious concern with the dimensions of a purely fictional landscape? Of the many possible explanations, I find three particularly persuasive. The first centers on the strong civic passions of sixteenth-century Dante scholars. These passions are apparent in nearly every study of Hell's terrain. When Landino first presents Manetti's plan in 1481, he not only praises the architect for his perspicuity, but also praises Florence for counting such a brilliant reader among its poets and artists. When the Luchese scholar Vellutello refutes these calculations, he takes the opportunity to mock the Florentine readers who accepted a "blind man" as their guide.[11] When Galileo lectures on Manetti's calculations, he speaks quite clearly as an advocate for the Florentine cause; his goal, he announces, is to refute Vellutello's "false calunnie" and to restore the honor of the "dottissima e nobilissima Accademia Fiorentina."[12] For both practitioners and spectators, the mapping of Hell was thus more than a dry academic discourse; it was a topic that excited political as much as philological fervor.

Another possible reason for infernal cartography's appeal is the prominence and popularity of terrestrial mapmaking during the same period. At the start of the sixteenth century, the study of the earth's surface had just entered a new, exciting phase. The recent translation and publication of Ptolemy's *Geographia* had reintroduced European cartographers to the science of projective geometry and set off a wave of experimentation. Cartographers like Gerhardus Mercator and Jo-

Figure 2. Map of Hell from Benivieni's *Dialogo circa el sito forma et misure dello inferno* (Florence, 1506). Courtesy of the Department of Special Collections, Stanford University Library.

CVMA

HERV in aco

diametro

sciarrui

acheronte fiu

limbo

luxuriosi

golosi

auari et prodighi

irosi

SITO ET FORMA DELLA

heretici

ciacco

violenti al prossimo
violenti a se stessi
violenti a dio alla natura all arte

minotauro

furati

nissuni fedeli
simoniaci
negromanti
baratteri
hipocriti
iadri
ingannatori
sismatici
falsatori

CENTRO DEL

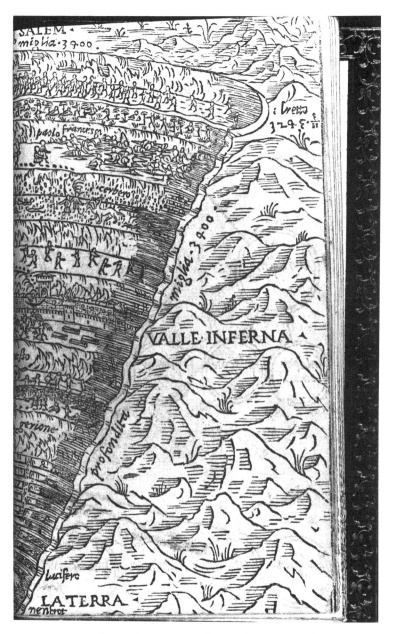

Figure 3. Map of Hell from *Dante col sito et forma dell'inferno tratta dalla istessa descrittione del poeta* (Aldine forgery, 1515). Courtesy of the Department of Special Collections, Stanford University Library.

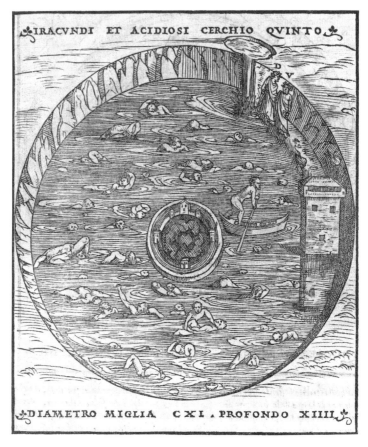

Figure 4. Overview of Hell's fifth circle from Vellutello (1544). Courtesy of the Department of Special Collections, Stanford University Library.

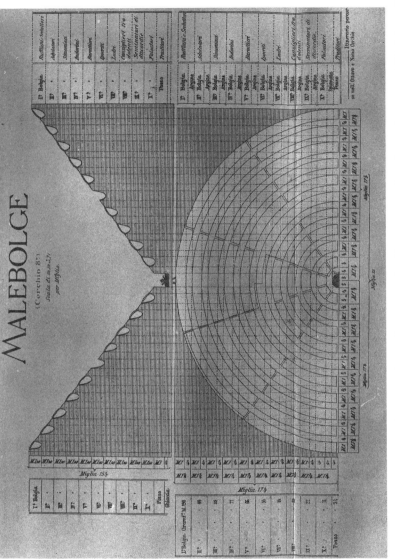

Figure 5. Cross section of the Malebolge from Agnelli's *Topo-cronografia* (1891). Courtesy of Division of Rare and Manuscript Collections, Carl A. Kroch Library, Cornell University.

hann Werner realized they could adapt Ptolemy's methods to twist the earth into a host of new shapes, from ovals to cordiforms, each with its own novel virtues. At the same time, of course, the great sea voyages of discovery were yielding new territories in need of representation. These innovations produced a fresh market for maps and fresh expectations. In the new order, mathematical rigor and objective measurement were held to be the map's essential properties—the very same properties that Galileo, Landino, and Vellutello claimed to find exhibited in Dante's description of the underworld.[13] One could thus argue that the maps of Hell simply extend into the world of fiction this much broader interest in accurate spatial representation: the scholars were mapping Dante's Hell as if they were passengers on an explorer's vessel.[14]

A third possible explanation for the rise of infernal cartography emphasizes the philosophical and aesthetic dimensions of measurement. For Renaissance humanists and artists, numerical measurement had an importance that went far beyond mere quantitative precision. Number was held to be the key not only to reproducing nature faithfully but also to perceiving and representing its harmony; it is through number and, more specifically, through proportion that the philosopher comprehends the unity of creation and that the painter manifests its beauty. This mathematical idealism is extremely clear in the work of Dante's Renaissance cartographers. Even a quick survey of their maps reveals a persistent emphasis on perfect ratios and ideal geometrical constructions. While one scholar presents Hell as an equilateral triangle sliced into ten equivalent wedges, another imagines Hell growing outward from its center in a series of symmetrically spaced circles. It is taken for granted by Landino, Galileo, and Manetti that the most harmoniously proportioned map is the one closest to their poet's vision.[15] Galileo's dedication to the *Dialogo dei massimi sistemi* might easily serve as the dedication to his lectures on the shape of Hell—in each case, his subject is the "excellent proportions" that are the trademark of divine craftsmanship:

Benché tutto quel che si legge [nel gran libro della natura], come fattura d'Artifice onnipotente, sia per ciò *proporzionatissimo*, quello nientedimeno è più spedito e più degno, ove maggiore, al nostro vedere, apparisce l'opera e l'artifizio.[16] (Emphasis mine)

And though whatever we read [in that great book of nature] is the creation of the omnipotent Craftsman, and is accordingly *excellently proportioned*, nevertheless that part is most suitable and worthy which makes His work and His craftsmanship most evident to our view.

Academic *campanilismo*, innovations in terrestrial cartography, and mathematical idealism all help to account for the peculiar popularity of infernal cartography in the Renaissance. Yet, as readers of Dante, it is important that we recognize a fundamental difference among these various explanations. Since the academic rivalries of the sixteenth century and the innovations of Mercator are foreign to Dante's experience, they are necessarily foreign to his conception of his poem. Thus when we emphasize such factors, we effectively diminish the authority of the mapmaker's work; we suggest, at least implicitly, that the popularity of mapmaking among shrewd and sophisticated scholars was essentially a historical accident—a peculiar quirk of fifteenth- and sixteenth-century tastes and concerns. Consideration of the Renaissance enthusiasm for ratio and proportion leads us in the opposite direction. For this attachment to idealized geometry is a bridge between medieval and Renaissance culture, a bridge that does not extend into our century.[17] Unlike Landino, Galileo, or Brunelleschi, we are not likely to leap at the hint of mathematical congruence. We are not likely to believe that numerical structure is the key to beauty or that a perfect mathematical order governs the cosmos. And this puts us, as readers of the *Comedy*, at a clear disadvantage. Everywhere in Dante's work we find evidence that he shares the Renaissance's fascination with ideal ratios and perfect proportions. We see it in the complex numerological structure of his poem, in his criticism of the work of other poets, in his astronomical excursuses, and in his observations about beauty.[18]

But does this mean that we should accept the cartographer's

approach as valid? Is it actually the case that Dante visualized the infernal terrain with geometrical precision? Unfortunately, the text's answer to this question is ambiguous. If we consult the early cantos of the *Inferno*, there is no evidence whatsoever of rigorous geometry. In the dark wood and in the circles of the Incontinent it is extremely difficult even to visualize the terrain's general shape, let alone measure its dimensions. Virgil may point "qua giù" and Dante may use the term "cerchio," but these vague hints are hardly sufficient guides to producing an accurate map. If we consult the final cantos, however, we find a persistent emphasis on number, measure, and proportion. In the last six cantos of the poem, there are no fewer than eight exacting measurements of the terrain and its inhabitants.

This final series of measurements has served as the basis for all rigorous studies of Hell's dimensions. For though there are several passages in the central cantos of the *Inferno* where the poet offers clear *qualitative* descriptions of the terrain's shape, it is only at the end of the poem that he provides *quantitative* estimates. So important are these measurements historically that they will be treated here at some length and with some care. To gauge their usefulness, I shall ask you to view them with the narrow but probing gaze of a cartographer.

Let us begin with the first two examples from cantos 29 and 30. The speaker in the first passage is Virgil, and his subject is the ninth ditch (bolge) of the eighth circle; the speaker in the second passage is the Florentine counterfeiter Maestro Adamo, and his subject is the tenth ditch:

> Pensa, se tu annoverar le credi,
> che miglia ventidue la valle volge.
> E già la luna è sotto i nostri piedi.
>
> (*Inf.* 29.8–10)

> Io sarei messo già per lo sentiero,
> cercando lui tra questa gente sconcia,

con tutto ch'ella volge undici miglia,
e men d'un mezzo di traverso non ci ha.
                    (*Inf.* 30.84–87)

Consider, if you think to count them, that the valley circles 22 miles;
and already the moon is beneath our feet.

I would have set out already on the road to seek him among this dis-
figured people, even though it is eleven miles around and not less than
half a mile across.

These two passages tell us directly about the size and shape
of the Malebolge's two smallest ditches: the ninth ditch is, we
learn, 22 miles in circumference, whereas the tenth has a cir-
cumference of eleven miles and is one-half mile in width. But
if we follow the advice of the venerable *Ottimo commento* and
"use geometry" to extrapolate, we can squeeze much more in-
formation from this cluster of measurements. The striking 2:1
proportion between the ninth and tenth ditches invites us to
project widths for the other eight.[19]

ditch	10	9	8	7	6 . . .
circumference (miles)	11	22	(44)	(88)	(176) . . .

No less tempting is the possibility of using these passages to
plot the travelers' position as they move toward Satan. If the
ninth ditch is 22 miles in circumference, it follows that its di-
ameter is seven miles. Thus when Virgil and Dante are stand-
ing in the ninth ditch listening to the severed head of Bertran
de Born, they should be $3\frac{1}{2}$ miles from Hell's central axis. Us-
ing our previous extrapolations, we can calculate the poet's
position at every stage of his journey through the Malebolge.

$$\frac{\text{Circumference}}{\text{Diameter (miles)}} = pi = \frac{22}{7}.$$

ditch	10	9	8	7	6 . . .
circumference	11	22	44	88	176 . . .
diameter	$\frac{7}{2}$	7	14	28	56 . . .
distance from center	$\frac{7}{4}$	$\frac{7}{2}$	7	14	28 . . .

Deriving a circle's diameter from its circumference is a relatively simple task, but it is worth noting that Dante has made the calculation particularly simple by employing the numbers 22 and 11.[20] Since the best estimate of *pi* was given in Dante's time by the fraction $^{22}/_7$, Dante's readers could determine the diameters of the 22-mile circle and the 11-mile circle effortlessly.[21] Had Dante chosen different circumferences for his ditches, the calculation of their diameters would have involved messy fractions—a circle with a 20-mile circumference would have, for example, a diameter of $6^4/_{11}$ miles and a radius of $3^4/_{22}$ miles. In choosing such convenient dimensions, Dante may be imitating Macrobius. In his *Commentary on the Dream of Scipio*, the Latin writer uses a similar circle to teach his readers about the art of extrapolation.

The diameter of every circle, when tripled with the addition of a seventh part, gives the measurement of the circumference in which it is enclosed; for example, if a diameter is *seven* inches long and you desire to know the length of the circumference, you triple seven, making twenty-one, and add a seventh part or one, and [thus we see that] the circumference of a circle whose diameter is *seven* inches is *twenty-two* inches. We could prove these statements by obvious geometrical processes were it not that we believe everyone assents and that we are anxious to keep this commentary reasonably brief.[22] (Emphasis mine)

More information about the terrain is provided when the travelers cross over the final ditch of the Malebolge and encounter the giants Antaeus and Nimrod. As Dante marvels at these huge, terrifying creatures, he repeatedly, even obsessively, measures their bodies: Nimrod is measured three times using three different measuring units; Antaeus is measured once.

> Noi procedemmo più avante allotta,
>   e venimmo ad Anteo, che ben cinque alle,
>   sanza la testa, uscìa fuor de la grotta.
>
> (*Inf.* 31.112–14)

We then proceeded farther on and came to Antaeus, who stood full five ells, not reckoning his head, above the rock.

Since Antaeus bends over to lower Dante into the central well containing Lake Cocytus, the measurement of that giant's height is a clue to the well's depth: the pit should be roughly half his height. But to calculate his height we have to employ another set of proportions: those of the human body. Dante has chosen, for some reason, to measure the giants only in segments—either a giant's head or a giant's headless torso. In the case of Antaeus, the calculation runs as follows:

$$\text{torso} = 5 \text{ ells};$$
$$\frac{\text{torso}}{\text{entire body}} = \frac{3}{8};$$
$$\text{Antaeus} = \frac{8}{3}(5 \text{ ells});$$
$$\text{central pit} = \frac{4}{3}(5 \text{ ells}).$$

When Dante reaches Satan in canto 34, he again carefully measures the enormous body, and he again uses proportions to do so.

> Lo 'mperador del doloroso regno
>   da mezzo 'l petto uscia fuor de la ghiaccia;
>   e più con un gigante io mi convegno,
> che i giganti non fan con le sue braccia:
>   vedi oggimai quant'esser dee quel tutto
>   ch'a così fatta parte si confaccia.
>
>   (*Inf.* 34.28–33)

The emperor of the woeful realm stood forth mid-breast out of the ice; and I in size compare better with a giant than giants with his arms: see now how huge that whole must be to correspond to such a part.

To see all of Satan ("quel tutto"), we must first compare Dante's height to the height of a giant. We must then use that proportion to estimate the length of Satan's arm, and then finally use the length of Satan's arm to estimate Satan's height:

$$\frac{\text{Giant's height}}{\text{Satan's arm}} = \frac{\text{Dante's height}}{\text{Giant's height}};$$

$$\text{Satan's height} = \frac{3 \, (\text{Giant's height})^2}{\text{Dante's height}}.$$

It is a complicated procedure, but one that Dante presents with particular urgency. The poet explicitly commands us to see "now" ("vedi oggimai") by means of the proportions that he weaves together.

As it turns out, quite a lot of information can be extracted from the eight measurements of the final cantos. With a few modest extrapolations, we can compute the circumferences and diameters of the various ditches of the Malebolge, the width of those ditches and their stone embankments, the height of Satan and the height of the giants that surround him, and the depth of the central well. It does indeed seem possible to map the infernal landscape, at least in the restricted context of the two final circles.

Renaissance cartographers did not settle, of course, for mapping only the Malebolge and Cocytus. The temptation to extend their maps to the rest of Hell was irresistible, and they found a variety of methods for determining the widths, depths, and diameters of the seven circles that Dante does not explicitly measure.[23] There is not much point in examining these calculations in detail, for though they are often wonderfully ingenious, they do not tell us much that is useful about Dante's poem. On the contrary, the attempts of Renaissance scholars to calculate the dimensions of upper Hell tend to obscure what is probably the most critical fact about Dante's measurements: their concentration in Hell's lowest circles. If we are to understand the function of measurement in the *Inferno*, we need first to take account of its place in the poem.

It should be noted at once that the dense clustering of measurements in the final cantos is not an accident. In the course of Dante's descent, there is a continuous evolution toward more objective and exacting descriptions of the terrain. When the travelers pass through the gates of Hell in canto 3, the shadowy allegorical landscape of the dark wood is exchanged for a more stable, but still obscure, terrain. As they descend further into Hell, the vague descriptions of slopes and circles give way to increasingly graphic portrayals of isolated landmarks. Still deeper in the descent, when the travelers cross into the city of Dis, Hell is revealed as a coherently organized space articulated according to a clear plan. At the midway point in canto 18, Dante gets his first aerial view of this ordered landscape. Finally, at the very end of the journey, Hell's terrain is measured out numerically and the travelers' position plotted precisely.[24]

This gradual progression from the confusion of the dark wood to the clarity of lower Hell is especially striking because it is so unexpected. The poet has chosen to represent the surface of the earth as a dreamlike space existing nowhere and everywhere, while representing the otherworldly landscape as a realistic physical place whose shape and location can be charted and measured. It is an odd choice, not only because it makes the familiar seem unfamiliar (and vice versa), but also because it overturns the pattern of the *Inferno*'s primary secular model: Virgil's narration of Aeneas's journey to the Elysian Fields. In *Aeneid* 6, the descent to the underworld begins at a well-defined spot on the earth's surface—the hollow caves at Cumae—and ends in an ambiguous landscape whose location is extremely difficult to pinpoint. The Latin poet suggests that the Elysian Fields are beneath the surface of the earth, yet he also notes that they possess their own sun and stars ("solemque suum sua sidera," *Aen.* 6.641). And while the Sibyl announces to Aeneas that it is easy to descend and difficult to return from the underworld ("facilis descensus Averno . . . sed revocare gradum . . . hoc opus, hic labor est," *Aen.* 6.126–29), Aeneas's return occurs instantly and effortlessly. Instead of climbing laboriously back to the surface as Dante does, Aeneas merely steps through the gate of false dreams. It is at the end rather than the beginning of the descent that the Trojan's journey edges closest to vision and illusion.

If the *Inferno* told the story of a pilgrim's unerring progression toward the truth, this inversion of the Virgilian pattern could be easily explained. Earth, we might conjecture, is represented as a confused, unreal landscape because earthly existence is, from the perspective of eternity, no more than an interval of passing shadows. As the pilgrim moves deeper and deeper into Hell, he gradually awakens from his spiritual slumber and comes to understand the system of God's justice. It is only at the end of the *Inferno* that the poet reveals the true order of Hell because it is only at the end of the journey that the scales fall from the pilgrim's eyes. The problem with this reading is that the *Inferno*'s trajectory is actually far more ambiguous. In many works of literature, the end may be a place where uncertainties are finally resolved and the risks of ironic reversal finally surpassed, but that is not the case in Dante's poem. On the contrary, it is toward the end of the *Inferno*, when Dante descends into the circles of fraud, that his own performance is put most at risk. In almost every ditch of the Malebolge there is the danger that Dante's poetry will be contaminated by its subject matter, that his prophecies, fictions, and literary borrowings will be revealed as deceptions, lies, and thefts. That measurement should emerge at the very nadir of this descent and become, almost immediately, a dominant mimetic device is thus no guarantee of its reliability. It might be that measurement is privileged by its context or damned by it; Dante may be inviting us to view measurement as the final, most accurate form of mimesis or as the most deceptive. We will be in a better position to decide between these alternatives when we have examined the measurements more closely and have traced infernal cartography's history beyond the Renaissance and into the twentieth century.

～⁓

Soon after Galileo's lectures on the shape of Hell, the practice of infernal cartography suffered a rapid decline in popularity. Just as it had flourished in a time when number, ratio, and proportion were central aesthetic and philosophical concerns, it languished as these concepts were pushed from center stage. No seventeenth- or eighteenth-century reader appears to have been interested enough in Dante's measurements to try his own hand at mapping Hell or to reevaluate critically the work of the Renaissance practitioners. Maps of Hell were intermittently produced in this period, but they were simply new drawings of old ideas—fresh sketches based entirely on Benivieni's and Vellutello's treatises.[25]

Then, just when infernal cartography threatened to fade entirely away, another shift in literary taste brought it back into fashion. With the rise of positivistic scholarship in the late nineteenth century, it again seemed important for readers to try to produce accurate maps. Some nineteenth-century readers, like Vaccheri and Michelangeli, devoted themselves to producing bold new maps of Hell, others to studying and refining the calculations of Landino, Vellutello, and Benivieni.[26] Even a partial list of the works produced by this new generation of mapmakers testifies to their energy and enthusiasm; between 1880 and 1900 they published four books on the shape of Hell, two brand-new editions of Benivieni's dialogue and Galileo's lectures, and a score of articles devoted to various vexing topographical questions, such as the configuration of the slope between the fifth and sixth circles and the orientation of Dante's spiraling descent through the Malebolge.[27]

But for all this activity, the nineteenth-century "renaissance" in cartography was little more than a last gasp. When infernal cartography first burst on the scene in the late fifteenth century, it attracted scholars of immense influence and authority. Landino had been heralded by Ficino as a "new Dante" and his commentary, along with that of Vellutello, had shaped the way most Renaissance readers approached the *Comedy*. The mapmakers who peddled their computations in the *Giornale dantesco* seem, by comparison, bit players. Some of them were even amateurs. Giovanni Agnelli, for example, the author of several articles on the infernal landscape and of the lavishly illustrated *Topo-cronografia di viaggio dantesco*, drew his beautiful maps of Hell and Purgatory (see Figure 5) during his free time at an institute for deaf-mutes. To secure an audience for their ideas, cartographers like Agnelli were dependent on the tolerance (if not approval) of a larger academic community, a tolerance that was quickly exhausted. Within 40 years of the publication of the *Topo-cronografia*, infernal mapmaking could be publicly dismissed as a pointless project pursued by "pathetic figures."[28]

Dantean cartography remains today a thoroughly discredited discipline. As a recent commentator happily observes, the "parasitic offshoots" of the Renaissance tradition have finally been stripped away from the "grande e genuino tronco della secolare esegesi dantesca."[29] But even this energetic pruning leaves one thorny question unresolved. What are we to make of the measurements that crowd the final cantos of the *Inferno*? If these measurements are not intended to show us the terrain of Hell, then they presumably have some other purpose.

Almost without exception, modern critics have argued that the purpose of the measurements is entirely stylistic, a function of the *Inferno*'s realism.[30] Dante measures the height of giants and the width of ditches and bridges not because their actual size is important, but in order to foster the illusion that Hell is a real place whose dimensions can be measured exactly. The measurements need not fit into a coherent pattern to achieve this effect—all that matters is the momentary impression created as the reader rushes through the narrative.

It is easy to see why some modern critics were inclined to dismiss the measurements as style without substance; exacting measurement could hardly satisfy the Crocean appetite for "poesia," for instance. Yet there is at least one group of modern readers, the authors of line-by-line commentaries, who might have been expected to take a more serious interest in Dante's hints about the terrain. Like their medieval and Renaissance predecessors, modern commentators display a remarkable faith in the underlying order of Dante's fiction and a persistent enthusiasm for implicit patterns. A revealing example of their interpretive approach is their response to the various astronomical images that crop up in the course of the poem. Commentators insist that these images are a coherent guide to the chronology of Dante's journey, and they spare no effort in proving their point. One recent commentator goes so far as to provide her readers with their own cut-out clocks for telling time in Hell and Purgatory.[31] Other commentators base precise calculations on the most loosely constructed images; a reference as vague as "e già la luna è sotto i nostri piedi" (and already the moon is beneath our feet) is commonly taken to imply that it is between one and two in the afternoon.[32]

If there is nothing wrong, *in principle*, about timing Dante's journey with such precision, then why do commentators insist that it is wrong, *in principle*, to study Dante's measurements of the physical terrain? Why do Bosco, Grandgent, and the *Enciclopedia Dantesca* advise us to ignore any symmetries and patterns that we might notice in the measurements? The inconsistent position of the commentators on the mapping and timing of Dante's journey is an indication that the real problem with cartography is not critical naiveté. To see what that problem is, we need to disobey the commentators' advice and pay very close attention to the measurements—closer attention than we have yet devoted.

Let us begin with Dante's measurement of Satan's body in canto 34. We noted earlier that Satan's height can be calculated by means of a proportion:

$$\text{Satan's height} = \frac{3\,(\text{Giant's height})^2}{\text{Dante's height}}.$$

Using estimates of Dante's and a giant's height, we can use this equation to derive a numerical estimate of Satan's height.[33]

$$\text{Satan's height} = \frac{3\,(70\ \text{ft.})^2}{6\ \text{ft.}} = 2{,}500\ \text{ft.}$$

According to Dante's measurement, Satan's body is approximately 2,500 feet tall. Much of this body is buried in the ice of Cocytus, but even the portion that rises above the frozen surface is enormous—a mass approaching the height of the World Trade Center. This result was reached by both Renaissance and nineteenth-century cartographers, and yet none gave more than passing attention to the troubles it creates.[34] One problem concerns the relative size of Satan and the three traitors who dangle from his mouth. In *Inferno* 34, these traitors are the subject of a long description that, even by Dante's standards, is unusually gruesome. We are shown their flayed bodies and writhing limbs with a graphic accuracy edging on sadism. As far as Dante's style is concerned, we reach in this passage a new low; we have sunk from lofty obscurity to grotesque immediacy. Yet even as the poet invites us to gaze upon the horribly tormented bodies of Cassius, Brutus, and Judas, he has placed those bodies far beyond the reach of his own sight. As the careful cartographer should realize, the traitors are much too far away from the travelers to be identified or described—at their height, they should be as insignificant a sight as a trio of deluded tourists waving from the top of the Empire State Building.

We run into even more serious problems when we try to accommodate Satan's vast bulk within the space granted him by the poet. To a casual reader it might appear that Cocytus is a vast, expansive region. There are, after all, two distinct occasions when the misty distances of lower Hell play tricks on the poet's vision. First, Dante mistakes the ring of giants for a ring of towers surrounding a walled city and asks his guide, "Maestro, dì, che terra è questa?" (Master, tell me, what town is this?; *Inf.* 31.21). Virgil corrects this error, pointing out to Dante that he has been deceived by distance.

> Però che tu trascorri
> per le tenebre troppo da la lungi,
> avvien che poi nel maginare abborri.
> Tu vedrai ben, se tu là ti congiungi,
> quanto 'l senso s'inganna di lontano.
> (*Inf.* 31.22–26)

It is because you peer through the darkness from too far off that you stray in your imagining; and when you reach the place you will see plainly how much the sense is deceived by distance.

Three cantos later, the poet is again having difficulty gauging the spaces of lower hell. As he draws toward Satan across the ice, he is asked by Virgil to look ahead ("dinanzi mira") and report what he sees. What Dante claims to observe is a shadowy, distant object resembling a windmill:

> Come quando una grossa nebbia spira,
>   o quando l'emisperio nostro annotta,
>   par di lungi un molin che 'l vento gira,
>   veder mi parve un tal dificio allotta.
>
>   (*Inf.* 34.4–7)

As, when a thick fog breathes, or when our hemisphere darkens to night, a mill which the wind turns appears from afar, such an edifice did I now seem to see.

All this fuss about distance and the tricks it plays should, by now, seem odd. Having studied the measurements of Hell, we know very well that here, in the final cantos, distances are extremely compressed. According to Dante's measurements, the total distance between the last ditch of the Malebolge and the giants and between the giants and Satan is only 1½ miles.[35] Thus, by the time Dante has crossed Cocytus, torn the hair from Bocca's head, listened to Ugolino's story, and tricked Alberigo, he should be within a few hundred yards of Satan's body; when Dante gets his first glance at the "distant windmill," he is standing less than five city blocks from a structure taller and more massive than the largest skyscraper.

An analogous set of difficulties is presented by Dante's measurement of Nimrod. In canto 31, the giant is measured three times using *palmi*, Frieslanders, and the "pina di San Pietro" as measuring units:

> La faccia sua mi parea lunga e grossa
>   come la pina di San Pietro a Roma,
>   e a sua proporzione eran l'altre ossa;

sì che la ripa, ch'era perizoma
    dal mezzo in giù, ne mostrava ben tanto
    di sovra, che di giugnere a la chioma
tre Frison s'averien dato mal vanto;
    però ch'i' ne vedea trenta gran palmi
    dal loco in giù dov' omo affibbia 'l manto.

(*Inf.* 31.58–66)

His face seemed to me as long and large as the pine-cone of St. Pe-
ter's at Rome, and his other bones were in proportion with it; so that
the bank, which was an apron to him from his middle downward,
showed us so much of him above, that three Frieslanders would have
barely reached to his hair; for I saw thirty great spans of him down
from the place where a man buckles his cloak.

If this clustering of measurements is supposed to allow us to
visualize Nimrod more clearly, then it fails in its purpose; the
multiple measurements tend to confuse rather than clarify our
impressions of his size. This is true both of a quick, casual
reading of the passage and of a more thorough analysis. For if
one takes the trouble to calculate the sizes of Nimrod's head
and headless torso, one finds that they do not match.[36]

Nimrod's torso = 3 Frieslanders = 18 ft.
Torso:face = 3:1; therefore Nimrod's face = 6 ft.
But Nimrod's face = pine-cone = 12 ft.

Dante may claim that Nimrod's head is proportioned to suit
his body ("e a sua *proporzione* eran l'altre ossa"), but in fact
Nimrod's head is twice as large as it should be. Once again, the
poet seems either to have inadvertently miscalculated or to have
deliberately toyed with our expectations. The latter alterna-
tive is especially credible in light of his treatment of the giants
Antaeus and Briareus. Both giants are represented in ways de-
vised to surprise a reader well acquainted with Ovid and Vir-
gil.[37] Although Antaeus was reputed to be invincible so long
as he remained in contact with the earth, Dante depicts An-
taeus half-buried in the rocky soil, a prisoner of the earth that
should empower him. And although Briareus was described as
a fantastic monster possessing fifty heads and one hundred arms,

Dante claims that he looks just like the other giants except for his fearsome expression: "È legato e fatto come questo, / salvo che più feroce par nel volto" (*Inf.* 31.104–5).

Still further evidence of contradiction and confusion is to be found in Dante's measurements of the ditches of the Malebolge. When first entering the Malebolge in canto 18, Dante describes a network of concentric ditches linked by little bridges ("ponticelli," *Inf.* 18.15) leading to a very wide and very deep central well ("un pozzo assai largo e profondo," *Inf.* 18.5). By the end of the travelers' journey through the Malebolge, enough information has been provided for us to calculate the dimensions of both the "ponticelli" and the "pozzo assai largo e profondo." Since we are told in canto 30 that the ninth ditch of the Malebolge is a half-mile across, it follows that the bridges spanning this ditch must also be a half-mile long. Similarly, since the giant Antaeus picks up Virgil and Dante and lowers them into the central well, it follows that the reach of the giant's arms should determine the depth of the pit; the pit should have a depth equal to no more than half the height of the 70-foot giant.[38] What we learn from these calculations is clearly inconsistent with the image of the terrain originally suggested by Dante in canto 18. According to the measurements, the *little* bridges are almost as long as the Brooklyn Bridge, and the *very deep* central well is barely twice the depth of a good-sized suburban swimming pool.

When Dante's measurements of the final circles are analyzed objectively, they reveal a terrain *dis*ordered by number and measure. Satan is too tall for the space allotted him, Nimrod's head is too big for his body, the little bridges of the Malebolge are too long, and the deep pit at the center of the Malebolge is too shallow. We do not notice this, of course, if we ignore the measurements as commentators advise us, and that, clearly, is the point of their advice. By dismissing calculation as a naive response to Dante's text, they avoid directly confronting the contradictions that careful mathematical analysis brings to light.

The treatment of Dante's measurements by Renaissance mapmakers and modern critics recalls the debate over the *Vita nuova*'s hidden symmetry. Two groups of critics disagree quite strongly about the deliberateness of a pattern, yet agree implicitly about the criteria for judging deliberateness: if a pattern is intentional it must be coherent and consistent; any structure that the poet creates must be carried out to perfection; in Dante's conception of his great system there is no room for error. Once again, I shall take a different approach and attempt to read the rough edges of Dante's pattern. In this case I shall ask whether the very point of Hell's measurements might be their consistent inconsistency.

To begin considering what might be at stake in mismeasurement, let us review the competing claims made by modern and Renaissance readers. In the eyes of modern commentators like Singleton and Bosco, measurement is a mark of the *Inferno*'s "realism." Number, they suggest, conveys an impression of arbitrariness, and arbitrariness, in turn, conveys an impression of reality. In the eyes of Dante's Renaissance commentators, by contrast, measurement serves a more symbolic function. The poet's use of number and proportion reflects, they assume, Hell's status as God's handiwork; the mathematical order of the terrain reveals the order of the mind that produced it. Of these two interpretations of measurement, the first accommodates mismeasurement far more readily. When the poet laboriously mismeasures Nimrod, when he claims to be tricked by the great distances of lower Hell, when he commands us to "see" Satan's impossibly oversized body, he is, we might suppose, laying a trap for the credulous members of his audience. If his tone at these moments of "precise" measurement seems teasing, it is because he knows how likely it is that his readers will misunderstand him and mistake his ironic exposure of "realism" for a genuine effort in that direction.[39] This is an appealing interpretive approach in part because it so neatly explains the restriction of measurement to the lowest circles of Hell: we are tricked (or enlightened) by the poet's spurious claims to mimetic precision in the very circles devoted to the punishment of fraud.[40]

Accommodating deliberate error within the Renaissance account of measurement is manifestly more difficult. To follow the lead of Landino and Galileo and to view Hell as the creation of a divine intellect, which establishes things perfectly, in proportion to one another, is to locate mismeasurement within a theological as well as a poetic context, and theology is an arena where Dante is not expected to play games. The rest of this chapter addresses this fundamental difficulty. I shall attempt to demonstrate that the poet's erring measurements do indeed have theological implications, and, more specifically, that his "mistakes" as a landscape architect bear directly on his pose as prophet and judge of his fellow man.

To pursue this reading, we shall need to shift, for the moment, the focus of our concern from the shape of the terrain to the shape of the human figures who inhabit it. Let us begin with Nimrod, the giant whose height is measured three times in canto 29. Nimrod, as Dante explains in the *De vulgari*, is the first major builder; he is the Babylonian king who in Genesis conceives the audacious idea of building into heaven itself.

Praesumpsit ergo in corde suo incurabilis homo, sub persuasione gigantis Nembroth, arte sua non solum superare naturam, sed etiam ipsum naturantem, qui Deus est; et cepit edificare turrim in Sennaar, que postea dicta est Babel, hoc est 'confusio,' per quam celum sperabat ascendere, intendens inscius non equare, sed suum superare Factorem.[41]

Incurable man, at the instigation of the giant Nimrod, presumed in his heart that he could not only outdo nature, but even the creator of nature himself, who is God, through his own art; and he began the building of a tower in Sennear, which was afterwards called Babel, that is, "confusion," by means of which he hoped to ascend into the heavens, intending unperceived not just to reach a level equal to, but even above, his own creator.

Like so many of the damned, Nimrod suffers a punishment that echoes his crime. God has planted him in the earth like a tower and has allowed him to speak only an incomprehensible language. Dante, too, tailors his response to the giant to suit his history. He compares Nimrod's face to a sculpture symbolizing artistic excess—the huge, gilded pine-cone[42]—and measures the architect repeatedly. In the Middle Ages, architecture was understood, above all else, to be an art of exacting measurement and just proportion; in medieval illuminations and on the tombs of master builders, architects are identified by the compasses and rulers that they clutch.[43] Since Nimrod is specifically a *failed* architect, it makes perfect sense that this most basic architectural principle should be abused. As Nimrod babbles, so his body is represented in a parodic babble of conflicting measurements. If this is actually Dante's intent, as I believe it is, then mismeasurement and misproportion communicate much more than a vague joke on the deceptive nature of mimesis; they are devices deployed to make a specific point about a specific sin—in this case, an architect's abuse of his craft.

   A second figure closely associated with the *Inferno*'s erring topography is Maestro Adamo: it is Adamo who, in canto 30, reports to Dante (and to us) the width and circumference of the Malebolge's tenth ditch. This is, again, a perversely appropriate association. Like Nimrod, Adamo practices an art that hinges on accurate measurement. He is a coiner and is in Hell for minting adulterated florins ("fiorini / ch'avevan tre carati di mondiglia," *Inf.* 30.89–90). Adamo's abuse of his art is figured in two distinct ways. First, for having coined *light* florins, he is afflicted with a *heavy* dropsy ("grave idropesi") that prevents him from moving even an inch in a hundred years ("S'io fossi pur di tanto ancor leggero / ch'i' potessi in cent'anni andare un'oncia"; *Inf.* 30.82–83). Second, Adamo's dropsy swells and distorts his body. Just as the architect's head is too big for his torso, so the coiner's face is too small for his paunch.

> La grave idropesì, che sì dispaia
>   le membra con l'omor che mal converte,
>   che 'l viso non risponde a la ventraia.
>   (*Inf.* 30.52–54)

The heavy dropsy which, with its ill-digested humor, so unmates the members that the face does not answer to the paunch.

This deformity takes on much greater importance because of the name the counterfeiter bears. Adam, the first and only perfect man, was made in God's image and likeness; Adamo is so disfigured by disease that he ceases even to look human. When Dante first notices the swollen forger, he compares him to a leg-bearing lute.

> Io vidi un, fatto a guisa di lëuto,
>   pur ch'elli avesse avuta l'anguinaia
>   tronca da l'altro che l'uomo ha forcuto.
>   (*Inf.* 30.49–51)

I saw one shaped like a lute, if only he had been cut short at the groin from the part where a man is forked.

Dante develops in his portrayals of Adamo and Nimrod a creative use for deformity and distortion: to depict an artisan who has abused the measures of his craft, Dante engages in artful mismeasurement. This strategic use of mensural error has, I believe, much wider applications. Many arts, besides coining and architecture, depend on just proportion and measurement, and two such arts are critical to Dante's project: the art of composing poetry and the art of administering justice.[44]

Poetry's links to measurement are rich and various. Meter is conceived of by Dante, and by other medieval theorists, as a matter of counting; indeed, the term Dante uses for "meter" in the *De vulgari* is the Latin term for "number"—*numerus* (2.5.7). Simile and metaphor are, from Aristotle onward, understood as types of proportion; rhyme, by contrast, is treated as a type of harmony.[45] All these forms of poetic measure are abused by Dante in his depiction of Nimrod and Adamo. Nimrod's cry—"Raphèl maì amècche zabì almi"—is as cacophonous as it is senseless and falls short of its proper length by two syllables (*Inf.* 31.67). Adamo's rhyme of "oncia" with "non ci ha" is the most flagrant (and most brilliant) example of *rima composta* in the entire *Comedy*.[46] The lute simile that describes Adamo's body is as deformed as the body it depicts; instead of creating a harmonious proportion between similar terms, it engenders a discordant opposition: a preeminent symbol of musical harmony—the lute—is likened to a body whose "armonia mirabile" has been hideously distorted.[47]

The ties between justice and measurement are even clearer. They are apparent both in iconographic representations of Justice—the blind goddess balancing a set of scales—and in more discursive discussions, like this passage from Aquinas's *Quaestiones disputatae de veritate*:

Et ideo primum ex quo pendet ratio omnis iustitiae est sapientia divini intellectus quae res constituit indebita proportione et ad se invidem et ad suam causam, in qua quidem proportione ratio iustitiae creatae constitit.

The primary thing upon which the essential nature of all justice depends is the wisdom of the divine intellect, which establishes things perfectly, in *proportion* to one another and to their cause. The essential nature of creative justice consists in this *proportion*.[48] (Emphasis mine)

Aristotle goes even further than such purely metaphorical formulations. In the *Nicomachean Ethics*, he not only asserts that "the just is a species of the proportionate," but also provides the mathematics necessary to put such a principle to work. We are taught in the *Ethics* how to choose the right type of proportion—geometrical or arithmetical—for various juridical situations and how to perform the necessary calculations.[49] So committed is Aristotle to this mathematical model that he traces the roots of the words "justice" and "judge" (*dikaion* and *dicastes*) back to the practice of geometry.

The just, then, is an intermediate, since the judge is so. Now the judge restores equality; it is as though there were a line divided into unequal parts, and he took away that by which the greater segment exceeds the half, and added it to the smaller segment. . . . The equal is intermediate between the greater and lesser line according to arithmetical proportion. It is for this reason also that it is called just (*dikaion*), because it is a division into two equal parts, just as if one were to call it *dichaion* and the judge (*dicastes*) is one who bisects (*dichastes*).[50]

Aristotle's interest in the analogy between measurement and justice should interest readers of the *Inferno* because the *Ethics* largely determines Hell's shape. It is from the *Ethics* that Dante borrows the term *contrapasso*, the categories *frode*, *incontinenza*, and *violenza*, and the basic idea of arranging crimes and punishments hierarchically.[51] Indeed, at times, Dante encourages us to view Hell as if it were a direct projection of Aristotle's text. Consider, for example, the exchange between Dante and Virgil that takes place in *Inferno* 11; after Dante admits to some confusion about the arrangement of sins in Hell, Virgil sharply upbraids him for forgetting the relevant section of the *Ethics*:

> "Perché tanto delira,"
> disse, "lo 'ngegno tuo da quel che sòle?
> o ver la mente dove altrove mira?
> Non ti rimembra di quelle parole
> con le quai la tua *Etica* pertratta
> le tre disposizion che 'l ciel non vole."
> (*Inf.* 11.76–81)

"Why does your wit so wander? And your mind, where does it gaze? Do you not remember the words with which your *Ethics* treats the three dispositions that Heaven wills not?"

Dante's dependence on Aristotle suggests a precise way of reading the measurements crowded into the *Inferno*'s final cantos: if the art of justice consists in finding the ideal proportion between crime and punishment, then we might expect the landscape of Hell—the physical expression of divine justice—to also be ideally proportioned. And yet, as we have seen, the actual shape of the landscape thoroughly refutes this expectation. The measurements of the Malebolge produce a semblance of order, but no more than a semblance. As we test Hell's proportions with increasing care, we find that Hell becomes increasingly confusing. This disappointment could lead us to reject the analogy between juridical and topographical order, or, alternatively, it could lead us to propose new approaches to reading the landscape. One reader might suggest, for example, that the erring measurements register the poet's doubts about the adequacy of divine justice; Dante is showing us, in Hell's contorted shape, how misproportioned God's punishments are. A second, more conservative reader might prefer to interpret Hell's disorder as a reflection of a purely infernal viewpoint; Hell seems deformed not because God is unjust, but because He is perceived that way by the damned. A third reader might conclude that it is specifically Dante's pretensions to judge his fellow man that are being parodied. It is not God's Hell that is deformed, but Dante's counterfeit.

The last of these alternatives is the one I find most attractive. Among its primary virtues is that it reminds us of an obvious but often neglected fact: no matter how vocally Dante asserts his rights as prophet and visionary, he is neither. The *Comedy* is not sacred scripture but a secular poem written by a secular poet. Dante knows that we know this, and his consciousness of our doubts is registered wherever those doubts might be most expected to matter. One thinks, for example, of the poet's greeting of Brunetto Latini in the circle of the Sodomites: "Siete voi qui, ser Brunetto?" The surprise in Dante's voice is brilliantly and difficultly ambiguous. It can be interpreted as proof of the poet's innocence and his enduring sorrow over Brunetto's sad fate, or it can be heard as part of a sublimely cruel joke: after damning his old teacher, Dante has the nerve to admit amazement over what he himself has done. The same cruel ambiguity is masterfully managed in canto 10 during the painful, fumbling conversation with the father of Guido Cavalcanti. Though the traveler acts as if he is amazed by the news of Guido's future, it is clear that the poet has gone out of his way to reveal his fate to the world; though Guido is not yet dead at the time of Dante's descent, it is strongly suggested that he will soon be coming to Hell—sent there in fiction, as in life, by his "primo amico." A third point where Dante's role as inventor edges uncomfortably close to the surface is his description of the bronze Sicilian bull in *Inferno* 27:

> Come 'l bue cicilian che mugghiò prima
>   col pianto di colui, e ciò fu dritto,
>   che l'avea temperato con sua lima,
> mugghiava con la voce de l'afflitto,
>   sì che, con tutto che fosse di rame,
>   pur el pareva dal dolor trafitto;
> così, per non aver via né forame
>   dal principio nel foco, in suo linguaggio
>   si convertian le parole grame.
>
>   (*Inf.* 27.7–15)

As the Sicilian bull (which bellowed first with the cry of him—and that was right—who had shaped it with his file) once bellowed with the voice of the victim, so that, though it was of brass, yet it seemed transfixed with pain: thus, having at first no course or outlet in the fire, the doleful words were changed into its language.

Though the most immediate function of this image is to recall Guido da Montefeltro's self-defeating deception, the image also informs against its creator. Dante shows us in this passage a diabolical instrument of mimesis and torture that is unmistakably modeled on his own. As the Sicilian craftsman finds himself swallowed up in his handiwork, so too, of course, does Dante as he journeys through the bowels of Hell; as the poet approves the punishment of his Sicilian double—"e ciò fu dritto"—he hints at the sadistic origins of his art.

Dante's taste for such scenes of dark self-reflection explains, I think, the prominence of Adamo and Nimrod. The sins of these two erring artists are precisely the sins Dante risks in his poem. To name those who will be damned and to measure out their "just" punishments for all eternity is to edge simultaneously toward fraud and hubris. That Dante cannot tear himself away from the counterfeiter's dialogue with Sinon, that he reencounters Nimrod's image on the terrace of pride, and that the final proportion of the *Inferno* links him to Satan and Hell's gigantic idolaters are all signs of the poet's identification with the damned. In the *Inferno*, as in *Paradise Lost*, an implicit symmetry between the poet's great aspirations and the aspirations of the first great sinners—Satan, Adam, and Nimrod—complicates the poem's more explicit claims to piety and prophetic truth.

This account of Hell's elusive order may seem grimmer and more anguished than I actually intend. For though I believe that Dante recognizes the ties between fallen angels and artists, and though I believe his erring measurements help establish this analogy, I do not think he finds the resemblance troubling, except when it serves his poetic purposes. Error, I feel, is staged neither in a spirit of humility—the broken symmetry of the Navaho rug—nor in the spirit of demonic narcissism. If I had to define the mood of Dante's essays in error, I would describe them as playful—a marshaling of fear and arrogance on behalf of art. This is, admittedly, a subjective response, but it is the one that has guided my analysis of Hell's erratic topography and that will guide the study of other types of error in subsequent chapters.

Chapter 3

The Learned Dante

Thick volumes piled at his elbow, manuscripts propped open before him, his brow furrowed in thought, Dante appears in Signorelli's famous portrait to be a man hemmed in by books (see Figure 6).[1] It is a faithful portrayal, if not of the poet's actual physiognomy, then at least of his popular image since the Middle Ages. In the scores of biographies and commentaries composed since his death, Dante has consistently been depicted as a gravely serious scholar. He is shown by Boccaccio, for example, reading right through a noisy Sienese parade, totally unaware of the athletic young men and beautiful girls swirling around him.[2] When Bruni, Villani, and Giovanni del Virgilio seek to praise the Florentine poet, they single out the depth of his erudition; he is, they insist, "a great scholar in almost every branch of learning," "the most learned of poets," and "the master of all sciences."[3] Dante's more recent admirers continue to endorse this tradition both in their new biographies of the poet and in their critical studies of his works. There are few, if any, postclassical authors whose writings have been more thoroughly sifted for echoes and allusions, few poets whose erudition has been more assiduously emulated. Even as the appeal of the scholarly apparatus seems, on the whole, to be waning in literary studies, *dantisti* continue to write monographs bristling with footnotes.[4]

Figure 6. Signorelli portrait of Dante, Orvieto Cathedral.

And yet there are moments when even the most admiring reader has to pause. One consequence of the exhaustive research into Dante's use of previous writers is the discovery of passages in which he appears to commit disappointingly rudimentary blunders, passages in which he seems to misconstrue, miscite, and mistranslate simple passages from very famous poems. Unlike the *Inferno*'s cartographic errors, which have had only a minor impact on modern Dante studies, these citational

vagaries have been the subject of increasingly intense scruti-
ny; they have been analyzed in numerous articles, reviews, and
monographs and, in the process, have helped stimulate ambi-
tious new theories about Dante's aims as a writer.[5] To take up
this topic is thus to enter into a discussion that touches on the
preoccupations and inhibitions not only of past generations of
readers, but also of those of the last two decades.

A complete survey of Dante's readerly errors and the re-
sponses they have provoked would require a book-length study.
But we can, I feel, gain a good sense of what is at stake in the
subject by considering *Inferno* 20 and *Purgatorio* 22: these can-
tos contain some of the most shocking instances of miscitation
in the *Comedy*, and the critical literature on them is particularly
rich and insightful. By plotting the responses of critics to these
cantos, we will have a good measure of how the interpretation
of this type of error has evolved, and in what ways it still re-
mains problematic. My aim here, as in the last chapter, is to
work from specific errors toward a broader reading of Dante's
poetic agenda, a reading focused in this case on the poet's claims
to interpretive authority, his relation to his pagan teachers, and
his use of allegory.

Inferno 20, the canto of the diviners, is a canto with lots of
talk and very little action. It is dominated by Virgil, who speaks
in monologue while Dante listens and occasionally asks ques-
tions. As the seers pass before the travelers, Virgil describes
their bodies with cruel objectivity and comments on their his-
tories and habits. It is in these peripheral remarks that the ci-
tational errors of *Inferno* 20 are lodged.

The first seer to be named is the Theban augur and general
Amphiaraus. Like the rest of the seers, Amphiaraus has had his
head twisted backwards, a fact that Virgil eventually points out
to Dante. First, however, he reminds his fellow poet of Am-
phiaraus's history. In particular, he recalls the seer's descent to
the underworld.

> Drizza la testa, drizza, e vedi a cui
> s'aperse a li occhi d'i Teban la terra;
> per ch'ei gridavan tutti: "Dove rui,
> Anfïarao? perché lasci la guerra?"
> E non restò di ruinare a valle
> fino a Minòs che ciascheduno afferra.
>
> (*Inf.* 20.31–36)

Raise, raise your head, and see him for whom the earth opened before the eyes of the Thebans, at which they all cried, "Where are you rushing, Amphiaraus? Why are you leaving the war?" Nor did he stop his headlong fall down to Minos, who seizes everyone.

The most famous account of this journey is to be found in Statius's *Thebaid*, a work Dante knows well and cites often, particularly in the *Inferno*. Yet the version Virgil delivers here differs substantially from Statius's. In these lines we are asked to view the general from the perspective of his soldiers and to enjoy their rude sarcastic cry, "'Dove rui, Anfïarao? perché lasci la guerra?'" Our vision of the seer is that of a coward fleeing the battlefield. This is not at all Statius's opinion of Amphiaraus or of his disappearance into the earth. In the *Thebaid*, that event is presented as a marvel to be admired, proof of Amphiaraus's peculiar virtues: it is because the seer is respected by Apollo that he is permitted to enter the underworld unharmed, riding on his chariot. The general's soldiers do not mock his departure; they are, rather, frightened and disturbed. The interrogative "Dove rui" belongs, in Statius's poem, not to an unruly mob but to the god Pluto, and he speaks not in contempt but in a spirit of wonderment:[6]

> "At tibi quos" inquit, "manes, qui limite praeceps
> non licito per inane ruis?"
>
> (*Theb.* 8.84–85)

"But what shall be thy fate," he cries, "who rushest headlong through the empty realm on a path forbidden?"

That the words of an astonished god should be so deformed in translation speaks to the essential problem with Virgil's representation of the Theban seer. The wonder, shock, and marvel of the *Thebaid* have been reduced to pathetic, embarrassing failure.

The same bias is apparent in Virgil's representation of the next two seers: a pair of figures who walk together through the Malebolge rubbing their backs and bellies against each other. One member of this ungainly couple is the famous Greek seer Tiresias, the other an obscure Latin seer named Arruns:

> Vedi Tiresia, che mutò sembiante
>   quando di maschio femmina divenne,
>   cangiandosi le membra tutte quante;
> e prima, poi, ribatter li convenne
>   li duo serpenti avvolti, con la verga,
>   che riavesse le maschili penne.
> Aronta è quel ch'al ventre li s'atterga,
>   che ne' monti di Luni, dove ronca
>   lo Carrarese che di sotto alberga,
> ebbe tra' bianchi marmi la spelonca
>   per sua dimora; onde a guardar le stelle
>   e 'l mar non li era la veduta tronca.
>
>   (*Inf.* 20.40–51)

See Tiresias, who changed semblance from male to female, transforming all his members; afterwards he had to strike again the two entwined serpents with his rod before he could resume his manly plumes. He that backs up to the other's belly is Arruns; in the hills of Luni where grubs the Carrarese, he had a cave for his abode among the white marbles, from which he could observe the stars and sea with unobstructed view.

The most surprising aspect of Tiresias's portrait is the particular biographical detail selected for inclusion. Though we might expect Virgil to recall one of Tiresias's graver prophecies, he has chosen to focus on a memorable but by no means characteristic event—the seer's sex-change. When this incident is reported in the *Metamorphoses*, it is a sign of the seer's special power. His loss and eventual recovery of his masculinity draws the attention of Juno and Jupiter and becomes, indirectly, the source of his prophetic gift.[7] Lifted out of its original context, and retold with a vulgar, dismissive emphasis, the incident seems tawdry and embarrassing—Tiresias caught with his pants down.

If the portrait of Tiresias is insensitive to the seer's status as a far-seeing prophet, and if it betrays a distressingly crude interest in the purely physical aspects of his transformation—Tiresias's *membra* and his *maschili penne*—it can at least be said to be essentially accurate as far as the "facts" are concerned. This is not true of the portrait of Arruns; in addition to mocking the seer, Virgil misplaces him. In *Inferno* 20, Arruns's home is a cave set in a picturesque hillside overlooking the Mediterranean; in the *Pharsalia*—the original source for Arruns's portrait—it is the deserted walls of a city. According to Lucan, Arruns lives in Lucca, not in Luni: "Arruns incoluit desertae moenia Lucae" (*Phar.* 1.586).

The last two portraits of tormented seers—those of Manto and Eurypylus—draw upon the *Aeneid* as a source-text. In *Aeneid* 10, Virgil interrupts his narration of Aeneas's struggles in Italy to explain that his hometown, Mantua, was founded by the Italian warrior Ocnus. Ocnus, according to Virgil, named the city after his mother Manto, the prophetic daughter of Tiresias.

> Ille etiam patriis agmen ciet Ocnus ab oris,
> fatidicae Mantus et Tusci filius amnis,
> qui *muros matrisque dedit tibi, Mantua, nomen.*
> (*Aen.* 10.198–200)

Then Ocnus came, who roused his company from the paternal waterways: a son of sibylline Manto and the Tuscan river. Mantua, it was he who *gave you walls and named you for his mother—Mantua.*

In *Inferno* 20, "Mantua" is also traced back to "Manto," but in Dante's poem Manto is a substantially different person. She is not a mother, but a *vergine cruda*; it is not her son who founds the city and names it in her honor, but a group of strangers who have heard that a solitary witch once lived and died in the Mantuan fens:

> Quindi passando la vergine cruda
>   vide terra, nel mezzo del pantano,
>   sanza coltura e d'abitanti nuda.
> Lì, per fuggire ogne consorzio umano,
>   ristette con suoi servi a far sue arti,
>   e visse, e vi lasciò suo corpo vano.
> Li uomini poi che 'ntorno erano sparti
>   s'accolsero a quel loco, ch'era forte
>   per lo pantan ch'avea da tutte parti.
> Fer la città sovra quell' ossa morte;
>   *e per colei che 'l loco prima elesse,*
>   *Mantua l'appellar* sanz' altra sorte.
>
> (*Inf.* 20.82–93)

The cruel virgin, passing that way, saw land in the middle of the fen, untilled and without inhabitants. There, to shun all human fellowship, she stopped with her servants to practice her arts, and lived, and left there her empty body. Afterwards the people who were scattered round about gathered to that place, which was strong because of the marsh it had on all sides. They built a city over those dead bones, *and for her who first chose the place they called it Mantua*, without other augury.

Eurypylus undergoes an even stranger transformation. A minor character in *Aeneid* 2, he is said to have carried a message from the temple at Delphi back to the Greek troops gathered at Troy's shore:

> Suspensi Eurypylum scitantem oracula Phoebi
> mittimus, isque adytis haec tristia dicta reportat:
> "sanguine placastis ventos et virgine caesa,
> cum primum Iliacas, Danai, venistis ad oras:
> sanguine quaerendi reditus animaque litandum
> Argolica."
>
> (*Aen.* 2.114–19)

Perplexed, we send Eurypylus to ask the oracle of Phoebus, and he brings back from the shrine these gloomy words: "With blood of a slain virgin ye appeased the winds, when first, O Greeks, ye came to the Ilian coasts; with blood must ye win your return and gain favor by an Argive life."

When Virgil speaks in Dante's poem about Eurypylus, he grants the minor messenger a beard and dark shoulders. He moves him from the shores of Troy back to Greece and, most importantly, turns him into a full-fledged prophet. It is Eurypylus who, along with Calchas, sets the date of the Greeks' departure from Aulis:

> Quel che da la gota
> porge la barba in su le spalle brune,
> fu—quando Grecia fu di maschi vòta,
> sì ch'a pena rimaser per le cune—
> augure, e diede 'l punto con Calcanta
> in Aulide a tagliar la prima fune.
> Euripilo ebbe nome.
>
> *(Inf.* 20.106–12)

That one, who spreads his beard down from his cheeks over his swarthy shoulders, was augur when Greece was left so empty of males that they scarcely remained for the cradles, and with Calchas he gave the moment for cutting the first cable at Aulis. Eurypylus was his name.

Virgil presents five seers in *Inferno* 20 derived from four different Latin epics, and in every case he either mistakes the tone of the text he is citing or contradicts some basic fact. For a classical poet, it is a curiously clumsy performance. Yet one would never guess this from Dante's reaction. Nothing that he says to Virgil during his long address indicates that he is in any way surprised or disturbed. At no point does he interrupt to ask whether Virgil has made a mistake or to challenge any of his claims. Though Virgil's errors may have given Dante good grounds for challenging his teacher's authority, that authority goes officially unchecked.

Up until 1960, there was a general, if implicit, consensus among scholars that whatever problems existed in *Inferno* 20 were as much the work of the real poet as of his fictional guide. Had Dante known the proper location of Arruns's home, had he realized that Eurypylus was a messenger and not an oracle, he would have written *Inferno* 20 differently. It was assumed that Dante's silence in the face of Virgil's blunders reflected a mistaken reading or misrecollection of his sources.[8] The task of scholars became, as a consequence, the explanation of such puzzling incomprehension. The articles in the *Enciclopedia Dantesca* on Eurypylus and Arruns, for example, hypothesize some kind of scribal blunder. The misrepresentation of Eurypylus is attributed to a scribe's substitution of *placasti* in place of *placastis* in Dante's copy of the *Aeneid*; the misplacing of Arruns's home is traced to a substitution of *Luni* for *Luca* and *monti* for *moenia* in Dante's copy of the *Pharsalia*.[9] That actual manuscripts containing such errors have not yet been located is treated as an annoying but by no means fatal problem: that Dante seems confused is proof enough that there was some confusion in the texts he was consulting.

In recent years, however, critics have tended to move in a different direction. Instead of seeking philological excuses for Dante's errors, critics are now more inclined to interpret such discrepancies as polemical deformations. An exemplary instance of this new approach is Hollander's article on *Inferno* 20, "The Tragedy of Divination."[10] Published in 1980, that essay argues that all the poet's apparent "errors" are both intentional and meaningful. Dante moves Arruns's home to the hills because "the clear view from the heights, which is nowhere in Lucan, speaks more forcibly of the character's failure." He changes Tiresias's *baculum* into a *verga* "to help facilitate his urge to turn Ovid's irreproachable seer into the merest of soothsayers." And he rewrites Amphiaraus's chariot ride out of a "desire to turn the hidden Christian [Statius] into an even more vehement opponent of divination than he already was on his own terms." Discrepancies and divergences that might once have seemed to diminish Dante's expertise as a reader now offer "further evidence that Dante knew classical text[s] better than some would allow, even well enough to leave us, his readers, dazzled and bewildered." Dante's silence does not represent a careless endorsement of Virgil's errors: it is, rather, a tacit invitation to the reader to notice the gaps and interpret them.

To move from the entries in the *Enciclopedia Dantesca* to the

"Tragedy of Divination" involves no small realignment in critical methodology. The philological method of Padoan, Kraus, and Ghisalberti works by isolating problems, labeling them as anomalies, and then knocking them out one by one with a series of ad hoc solutions. Hollander's method, by contrast, consists in fitting the problems in the text into a pattern that can then be interpreted for its intent. Divergence and anomaly are recuperated by the action of generalization and thematization; it is a method closer to allegoresis than philology, and it is the method that I, too, employed when analyzing Hell's topographic errors. A second telling difference lies in the models of literary authority postulated by the two approaches. Implicit in the arguments of the philologists is the assumption that Dante relates to his classical teachers much as the modern philologist relates to Dante. In their accounts, the poet borrows the light of Virgil, Statius, and Lucan by demonstrating his long and devoted study of their works. He gains his readers' respect by proving that he knows the classical writers backward and forward and by claiming a place in the great tradition they established. Thus a critic like Stocchi notes the occasional infidelity but moves quickly to Dante's defense: Dante is, he claims,

[un] lettore di classici più attento e più corretto che non molti dei suoi contemporanei; un confronto, poniamo con il commento latino ai *Documento d'Amore* di Francesco da Barberino può dare la misura, per contrasto, del suo acume e della generale correttezza delle sue citazione.[11]

[a] reader of the classics more attentive and accurate than many of his contemporaries; if we contrast his work with Francesco da Barberino's Latin commentary on the *Documento d'Amore*, we can take the measure of the acuity and general accuracy of Dante's citations.

Critics like Hollander argue for a more complex account of literary history and the rhythms of influence and authority. While they acknowledge Dante's explicit pose as a devoted reader, they insist that it is just a pose. Even as the poet pretends to cite his sources accurately, he is actively engaged in rewriting them. Dante is out to alter and subdue the great classical tradition rather than merely to derive his authority from it. Indeed, Dante even expects his most alert readers to notice his distortions and to accept them. Dante wants us, so the argument runs, to recognize the immense liberties he is taking.

This bellicose model of miscitation works particularly well in *Inferno* 20 because Dante's pose as a devoted reader is so theatrically overstated. Throughout the canto—but particularly during the portraits of the Virgilian seers—Dante plays up his respect for his teacher with suspicious enthusiasm. Consider again the section of Eurypylus's portrait, quoted above. As we noted before, there are at least three different errors in this passage: Dante condemns Eurypylus for a crime he never committed; he links him to a character with whom he was never involved; and he ties him to an event with which he had nothing to do. Now consider the final section of the seer's portrait, where Virgil turns to Dante to comment on his readerly expertise:

> Euripilo ebbe nome, e così 'l canta
> l'alta mia tragedìa in alcun loco:
> *ben lo sai tu che la sai tutta quanta.*
> (*Inf.* 20.112–14)

Eurypylus was his name, and thus my high Tragedy sings of him in a certain passage—*as you know well, who know the whole of it.*

Viewed in isolation, this passage might appear to reinforce a "humanist" model of authority: Dante, speaking through Virgil, praises himself for knowing all of Virgil's *alta tragedìa.* Set in its context, however, the passage has a far more ambivalent effect. The incongruity between the self-praise and the poor performance is so extreme that Dante's celebration of his scholarship arouses distrust. How can Dante know the *Aeneid* "tutta quanta," how can he be the Latin poet's devoted student, if his citations betray such willful indifference to the original text? The citing of Eurypylus is not some conventional display of erudition—the well-placed, unctuous footnote[12]—it is a troubled and troubling one.

Closer analysis of the original passage naming Eurypylus makes Dante's use of the Greek "seer" seem even stranger.

> "Saepe fugam Danai Troia cupiere relicta
> moliri et longo fessi discedere bello;
> fecissentque utinam! saepe illos aspera ponti
> interclusit hiems et terruit Auster euntis. . . .
> . . . suspensi Eurypylum scitantem oracula Phoebi
> mittimus, isque adytis haec tristia dicta reportat:
> 'sanguine placastis ventos et virgine caesa,
> cum primum Iliacas, Danai, venistis ad oras:
> sanguine quaerendi reditus animaque litandum
> Argolica.'"
>
> (Aen. 2.108–11, 114–19)

"Often the Greeks longed to quit Troy, compass a retreat, and depart, weary with the long war; and oh that they had done so! Often a fierce tempest of the deep cut them off and the gale scared them from going. . . . Perplexed, we send Eurypylus to ask the oracle of Phoebus, and he brings back from the shrine these gloomy words: 'With blood of a slain virgin ye appeased the winds, when first, O Greeks, ye came to the Ilian coasts; with blood must ye win your return and gain favor by an Argive life.'"

The quotation marks bracketing this passage indicate that the primary narrator—Aeneas—is quoting a secondary speaker—Sinon. Dante cites this passage as if it were no different from any other in the *Aeneid*, yet because it originates with Sinon it has a very special status: it is, even within the *Aeneid*, a lie. Contrary to Sinon's claims, the Greek forces had not given up hope of conquering Troy; they had not waited wearily for the winds to change; they had not sent a messenger to Apollo's oracle; nor had they listened to any dire prophecy pronounced from his lips. The entire story is concocted to dupe the Trojans into taking the Trojan horse within their walls. Since Eurypylus is named solely in this fraudulent tale, his status in the *Aeneid* is uniquely uncertain.[13] He could be a real Greek soldier set into a deceptive fiction by Sinon, or he could be completely a figment of the famous liar's imagination. This lack of even a secure fictional claim to historic reality should probably disqualify Eurypylus for inclusion in the *Inferno*, yet there he is marching alongside Amphiaraus, Tiresias, Asdente, and Michael Scot. Dante is either an "expert" reader who has forgotten how problematic Sinon's speech is, or he is an expert reader who has recognized the creative possibilities of quoting liars.

We run into analogous problems when analyzing Manto's portrait. After describing how the seer came to give her name to Mantua, Virgil advises Dante that everything he has just said about her is absolutely true, and that no other version should be trusted. Any other claims made about Manto and Mantua are, he asserts, "lies":

> "Però t'assenno che, se tu mai odi
> originar la mia terra altrimenti,
> la verità nulla menzogna frodi."
> E io: "Maestro, i tuoi ragionamenti
> mi son sì certi e prendon sì mia fede,
> che li altri mi sarien carboni spenti."
> (*Inf.* 20.97–102)

"Therefore I charge you, if you ever hear a different origin given to my city, do not let such a lie defraud the truth." And I, "Master, your words are to me so certain and do so hold my confidence, that all others would be to me as dead coals."

Among the other versions that Dante just *might* hear is, of course, *Aeneid* 10.198–200. This is the passage that authoritatively establishes the connection between Manto and Mantua, and it is the passage Dante relies on when composing Virgil's infernal monologue.[14] But the two versions are *not*, we recall, consistent. The *Comedy*'s Manto is substantially different from the *Aeneid*'s—she is a virgin, not a mother—and she has very different ties to the city: Mantua is not founded by her son, it is merely the place where she drops dead. If all rival accounts of the city's founding are "lying frauds," then surely the *Aeneid* must fall into that category as well. Virgil, it would appear, is made to speak in the *Inferno* against his own poem.

This is a daring move for Dante to make. Fiction asks of its readers a suspension of disbelief that is always extremely fragile. Doubts once awakened are hard to silence, and having been raised about one work they spread quickly to others.[15] If the history told in the *Aeneid* can be called a "lie," then why can't the same ugly word be applied to the version recounted in the *Comedy*? How can Dante presume to correct his own best source? What right does one poet have to refute the fables told by another?

The questions that Hollander's analysis provokes are broader and more unsettling than those typically posed by strictly philological studies. To set out in search of contradictions is to set out along a slippery slope. Hollander does not, however, allow things to slide too far out of control, and he does not conclude his reading of *Inferno* 20 with a mere disclosure of crisis. Instead, he postulates an answer that by now is virtually canonical in studies of Dantean allusion: Dante is free to miscite his classical predecessors, mock their heroes, label their poems lies, because as a Christian writer he does not ultimately derive his authority from a secular, pagan tradition. The puzzles and conundrums that so bother the philologists actually work to Dante's advantage, for they signal his literary and ethical independence from his pagan teachers. The crisis turns out, in the end, not to undercut Dante's authority but to shore it up, to show us that he is always in control and insistent that we see that.

The dialectical movement of Hollander's argument from stasis to crisis to a new, more secure stasis is reflected in many other branches of Dante studies as well. Against the sometimes vocal objections of traditional scholars, irony, disorder, and contradiction have come to play increasingly prominent roles in critical treatments of the *Comedy*, especially those produced in this country. The tolerance, even enthusiasm, for crisis and aporia registered in literary studies at large has inevitably come to shape the way Dante and other medieval poets are read. Yet this shift in emphasis has not fundamentally shaken Dante's reputation for didactic zeal and high moral seriousness. On the contrary, perhaps in an effort to constrain and delimit newly discovered tensions, recent critics have tended to place an even greater emphasis on the *Comedy*'s theological imperatives than had been done previously. Dante has not become more self-ironic in the last 30 years; he has simply become more ironic about *other* writers, thinkers, and traditions.[16]

～

Purgatorio 22 contains fewer classical allusions than *Inferno* 20, but it has played an even more prominent role in discussions of Dante's citational methods.[17] The primary reason for this is the canto's subject matter: the story of Statius's secret conversion. According to *Purgatorio* 22, the pagan poet is saved from sin and converted to Christ's teachings by meditating on the *Aeneid* and the *Eclogues*. This story is naturally of great interest to students of Dantean allusion because the poet explicitly announces a saving role for secular poetry and because he does so without either direct precedent or historical evidence. Though there are many legends of pagans secretly converted, though there are even legends in which poetry is the instrument of salvation, there are no recorded legends in which the Silver Latin poet is saved by reading the *Aeneid*—in fact, no legends in which he is saved at all. For some reason, Dante has rewritten history to make a place for Statius in paradise even as he sends Virgil back to the underworld.

There is also a second motive for the canto's recent popularity: like *Inferno* 20, *Purgatorio* 22 is a canto in which Dante apparently miscites his sources. The problematic section is Statius's discussion of his former sin and his explanation of how two lines from *Aeneid* 3—"Quid non mortalia pectora cogis / auri sacra fames"—cured him of prodigality.

> Or sappi ch'avarizia fu partita
> troppo da me, e questa dismisura
> migliaia di lunari hanno punita.
> E se non fosse ch'io drizzai mia cura,
> quand' io intesi là dove tu chiame,
> crucciato quasi a l'umana natura:

"Perché non reggi tu, o sacra fame
de l'oro, l'appetito de' mortali?"[18]
voltando sentirei le giostre grame.

(*Purg.* 22.34–42)

Now know that avarice was too far parted from me, and this want of measure thousands of courses of the moon have punished; and were it not that I set right my care, when I gave heed to the lines where you exclaim, angered as it were against human nature: *"Why, O sacred hunger for gold, do you not govern the appetites of mortals?"* at the rolling should I feel the grievous jousts.

Placing Virgil's Latin and Statius's Italian side by side, one does not immediately notice anything odd or surprising. For every phrase in the Latin original, Dante has found, it appears, a close Italian equivalent:

quid = perché = why;
cogis (cogere) = reggi (reggere) = control, confine;
mortalia pectora = appetito di mortali = appetite of mortals;
auri sacra fames = sacra fame di l'oro = sacred hunger for gold.

But if Dante has managed to translate each isolated phrase correctly, he has nonetheless mistranslated the passage. Two key words—*sacer* and *cogere*—are subject to two alternative translations. In classical Latin, *sacer* can mean "sacred," but it can also mean "accursed"; the verb *cogere* can signify an act of restriction or confinement, but it can also suggest forward driving movement—an act of compulsion. As translator, Dante opts for one set of alternatives; readers familiar with *Aeneid* 3 and the story of Polydorus's murder will realize that these are the *wrong* alternatives.

Hunc Polydorum auri quondam cum pondere magno
infelix Priamus furtim mandarat alendum
Treicio regi, cum iam diffideret armis
Dardaniae cingique urbem obsidione videret.
ille, ut opes fractae Teucrum et Fortuna recessit,
res Agamemnonias victriciaque arma secutus

fas omne abrumpit: Polydorum obtruncat, et auro
vi potitur. *Quid non mortalia pectora cogis,*
auri sacra fames!

(*Aen.* 3.49–57)

This Polydorus, with great weight of gold, luckless Priam had once sent in secret to be reared by the Thracian king, when he now mistrusted the arms of Dardania, and saw the city girt with siege. When the power of Troy was crushed and Fortune withdrew, the Thracian, following Agamemnon's cause and triumphant arms, severs every sacred tie, slays Polydorus, and takes the gold perforce. *To what dost thou not drive the hearts of men, O accursed hunger for gold!*

The interrogative *quid* does not, in this case, ask "why" but "where." The verb *cogere* does not suggest constraint but compulsion. And, most importantly, the adjective *sacer* does not mean "sacred" or "holy" but "accursed." The proper translation is thus "*Where*, O *accursed* hunger for gold, do you not *drive* the appetites of mortals," rather than "*Why*, O *sacred* hunger for gold, do you not *control* the appetites of mortals." Virgil is decrying not prodigality, but the contrary sin of avarice.[19]

Unsympathetic readers like the Renaissance humanist Niccolò Niccoli have cited Statius's error as evidence of Dante's poor education in the classics and his general sloppiness.[20] They have noted that such an egregious blunder would be embarrassing in a schoolboy, let alone in a poet who presents himself as the master reader and heir triumphant of the Latin epic tradition. Dante's admirers have fended off such attacks using the same two strategies analyzed in the last section. They have alternatively denied that Dante mistranslates *Aeneid* 3.56–57 and insisted that his mistranslation of the passage is entirely deliberate.[21]

Those who deny that any distortion takes place in *Purgatorio* 22 have relied primarily on philological arguments. If the text is confusing, they say, it is not Dante's fault but the fault of his scribes, "most of whom," writes Bruni, "are ignorant dolts."[22] The most authoritative exponent of this approach is Petrocchi, who argues for the following emendation: in place of "*Perché* non reggi tu," he would substitute *"Per che* non reggi tu."[23] The addition of that single space between the first two syllables allows for a totally different translation of Dante's passage, one that accurately captures the meaning of the original Virgilian passage:

$$quid \ = \ per \ che \ = \ \text{to what;}$$
$$cogere \ = \ reggere \ = \ \text{to drive;}$$
$$sacer \ = \ sacro \ = \ \text{accursed.}$$

This rendering of 22.40–41 has won wide acceptance, appearing not only in the Edizione Nazionale of the Società dantesca but also in the editions of Sapegno and Singleton. Yet as skeptical readers have noted with increasing force and frequency, Petrocchi's corrective emendation rests on several very questionable glosses. Apart from the contested passage, nowhere in the *Comedy* or in any of Dante's other writings does *sacro* mean "accursed," nor is there any other instance of *reggere* used to suggest "compulsion." And even if we are willing to accept such anomalous interpretations of these terms, we are still left with a serious problem: Statius is guilty of prodigality, yet *Aeneid* 3.56–57 is an attack on avarice.

The readers who have pointed out these problems generally do so to justify their pursuit of a different solution altogether. After dismissing Petrocchi's emendation as implausible, they argue that Dante is well aware of the divergence between *Purgatorio* 22.40–41 and *Aeneid* 3.56–57 and that he is not bothered by it. He is finding in *Aeneid* 3 a "concealed moral significance."[24] Dante is entitled to do this because, as a Christian exegete, he has the right to "spoil the Egyptians"—to take from pagan texts what is useful toward his own salvation, even if it means doing violence to the original author's intent. Critics favoring this form of explanation like to emphasize the sophistication of Dante's approach: they often label Dante's rewriting of *Aeneid* 3 "allegorical"; they tend to place quotation marks around the term "mistranslation" and to use less pejorative phrases such as "misreading."[25]

This alternative response to Dante's "'mistranslation'" of *Aeneid* 3.56–57 finds strong doctrinal and historical support. Dante wrote during a period noted for its active, aggressive forms of interpretation. The metamorphosis that Ovid's *Metamorphoses* suffered at the hands of writers like Bersuire is well known, as are Philo's and Origen's sanitizing explications of the Song of Songs.[26] Virgil was himself one of the writers most often subject to such redemptive appropriations. His fourth eclogue, with its talk of a Virgin and a miraculous birth, was routinely glossed as a prophecy foretelling the birth of Christ.[27] In an extreme yet nonetheless revelatory moment, Abelard grants the fourth eclogue a higher authority than the prophecies of the Old Testament.[28]

This tradition, we recall, features prominently in the second half of Statius's fictive autobiography. After discussing his renunciation of prodigality, the Roman poet moves on to describe his conversion from paganism to Christianity. Virgil's poetry, once again, helps save Statius, and in this case the saving passage is from the "prophetic" fourth eclogue:

> Saeclorum nascitur ordo.
> iam redit et Virgo, redeunt Saturnia regna,
> iam nova progenies caelo demittitur alto.
>
> (*Ecl.* 4.5–7)

> "Tu prima m'inviasti
> verso Parnaso a ber ne le sue grotte,
> e prima appresso Dio m'alluminasti.
> Facesti come quei che va di notte,
>   che porta il lume dietro e sé non giova,
>   ma dopo sé fa le persone dotte,
> quando dicesti: '*Secol si rinova;*
>   *torna giustizia e primo tempo umano,*
>   *e progenïe scende da ciel nova.*'
> Per te poeta fui, per te cristiano."
>
> (*Purg.* 22.64–73)

The line of the centuries begins anew. Now the Virgin returns, the reign of Saturn returns; now a new generation descends from heaven on high.

"You it was who first sent me toward Parnassus to drink in its caves, and you who did first light me on to God. You were like one who goes by night and carries the light behind him and profits not himself, but makes those wise who follow him, when you said, '*The ages are renewed; Justice returns and the first age of man, and a new progeny descends from heaven.*' Through you I was a poet, through you a Christian."

Though no direct translational error occurs here, as it does in lines 40–41, Statius nonetheless misinterprets Virgil: Statius is converted by Eclogue 4 because he identifies the vague references to the Virgin, the Miraculous Birth, and the New Order as elements in a proto-Christian prophecy, even though Virgil himself could not have understood his words in this way. As Dante points out in the *Monarchia*, Virgil's fourth eclogue elaborates a political rather than a religious allegory; it is about secular justice and Augustan ambition, not the "empire" of God:

"Virgo" namque vocabatur Iustitia, quam etiam Astream vocabant; "Saturnia regna" dicebant optima tempora, que etiam "aurea" nuncupabant. (*Mon.* 1.11.1)

By "Virgin" he [Virgil] meant Justice, who was also called Astraea. By "Saturnian kingdoms" he meant the best ages, which were also called "golden."

Statius's Christian reading of Eclogue 4 does much to make his earlier erring translation of *Aeneid* 3 seem deliberate. It is, one could argue, a small step between misreading a line of verse and misidentifying a poet's subject matter. In each case, the original author's understanding of his own writing is overridden by a reader who knows better. In each case, the will of the reader takes precedence over that of the writer who precedes him.

Up to this point I have done my best to make a persuasive case for the theory of "corrective misreading" that has recently been articulated by Hollander, Barolini, Shoaf, and other students of *Inferno* 20 and *Purgatorio* 22. I now want to press the potential limitations of this approach.

One vulnerability is the theory's functionalist foundation, the assumption that the "'errors'" of these cantos serve a well-defined didactic end and that they are intended to establish the authority of Christian teachings. If this was, in fact, Dante's goal in "misreading" Virgil, then he was sadly unsuccessful in realizing it. In the period when the *Comedy*'s audience might conceivably have been swayed by its moral philosophy, Dante's lesson fell on deaf ears. The characteristic response of medieval and Renaissance readers to *Inferno* 20 and *Purgatorio* 22 was not a renewed faith in the superiority of Christian values, but distress at the Christian poet's apparent bungling as a classicist. Bruni and others register real discomfort when they have to defend their poet from the charge of incompetence. Had Dante been primarily concerned with saving souls, he would have been better off being more direct. If he wanted to discredit pagan prophecy, he might merely have focused on some of the more horrific seers and soothsayers who populate classical poetry; an accurate summary of Erichtho's bloody sacrifices in the *Pharsalia* would, for example, have been easily as effective as a biased portrayal of Arruns or Amphiaraus.

A second, related problem with the theory is its failure to account adequately for the disturbing nature of Dante's "corrective" procedure. Dante might have hoped that his most sophisticated readers would eventually recognize the larger aims of his strategic deformations, but he cannot have believed that his strategy would be immediately self-evident. If it were *easy* to opt for an allegorical resolution of his apparent errors, then sober philologists like Petrocchi and Singleton would not have accepted highly implausible emendations. Whether or not one decides that Statius's misreading ultimately makes sense, one needs to pass through a difficult initial period. First impressions matter, and in this case a reader can hardly avoid the initial impression that Dante is either a poor translator or very forgetful. By remaining silent about his method, Dante effectively encourages us to misread his misreading.

The final and, I think, most telling difficulty with the notion of "corrective misreading" is contextual. If it were indeed the case that miscitation represented an aggressive effort on Dante's part to shore up his authority over Virgil and other erring pagan poets, then we would expect the sections of the *Comedy* containing such polemical distortions to be highly controlled and consistent. In order to draw our attention to the *corrective* aspect of his "misreadings," Dante should convince us that he is otherwise in command of the situation. But this is not, in fact, what he does. Far from being a careful, prudent poet in *Purgatorio* 22 and *Inferno* 20, Dante falls (or leaps) into several striking inconsistencies.

The contradiction in *Purgatorio* 22 is well known and has already vexed scholars for several centuries. As soon as Statius finishes recounting his life story, he asks Virgil which pagans are damned and where they are to be found. Virgil responds by listing the famous poets who inhabit Limbo and then, almost as an afterthought, proceeds to list the characters from Statius's poem who dwell there as well.

> Quivi si veggion de le genti tue
> Antigone, Deïfile e Argia,
> e Ismene sì trista come fue.
> Védeisi quella che mostrò Langia;
> èvvi la figlia di Tiresia, e Teti,
> e con le suore sue Deïdamia.
> (*Purg.* 22.109–14)

There of your own people are seen Antigone, Deiphyle, Argia, and Ismene sad still as she was. There she is seen who showed Langia; there is the daughter of Tiresias and Thetis and Deidamia with her sisters.

The puzzling figure in this list is, of course, "la figlia di Tiresia." According to Statius's two major poems—the *Thebaid* and *Achilleid*—Tiresias has only one daughter: the prophetess Manto. Yet Manto cannot possibly be an inhabitant of Limbo; as we know from *Inferno* 20, Manto walks among the false seers of the Malebolge.[29]

Manto's misplacement is an error entirely of Dante's making. It is a contradiction not between different texts and traditions, but within the system of the *Comedy* itself. It is a contradiction timed, moreover, to make us feel especially uncomfortable. If there is a single, central subject for Statius's and Virgil's conversation in Purgatory, it is the rules governing the placement of souls. Virgil wants to know why Statius, a pagan, is saved, and why he should have ended up on the terrace of Avarice. Statius in turn wants to know if the other great pagan poets are damned, and if so, where in Hell they are located. From Statius we learn how the penitent are released from their sufferings and how contrary sins are expurgated on the same terrace. From Virgil we learn how it is that he, a lost soul, has been temporarily permitted to enter Purgatory. All this attention to the rules and regulations of the mountain leads us to expect consistency in the way judgments are delivered—an expectation that is impossible to satisfy concerning Manto. If Manto is a prophetess, and if prophecy is a crime, then how can Manto be located in Limbo among the virtuous pagans? If, on the other hand, Manto is a "good" prophet, then why is so much space devoted to describing her punishment in the circle of the false seers? When it comes to judging Manto, Dante is awkwardly unsure of himself.

Inferno 20 contains a different type of inconsistency, one that critics have not, to my knowledge, documented, but one that is, if anything, more impressive than Manto's contradictory placement. The first hint of it comes in the passage naming the modern seers who stroll through Hell.

> Quell' altro che ne' fianchi è così poco,
>   Michele Scotto fu, che veramente
>   de le magiche frode seppe 'l gioco.
> Vedi Guido Bonatti; vedi Asdente,
>   ch'avere inteso al cuoio e a lo spago
>   ora vorrebbe, ma tardi si pente.
> Vedi le triste che lasciaron l'ago,
>   la spuola e 'l fuso, e fecersi 'ndivine;
>   fecer malie con erbe e con imago.
>   (*Inf.* 20.115–23)

That other who is so spare in the flanks was Michael Scot, who truly knew the game of magic frauds. See Guido Bonatti; see Asdente, who now wishes he had attended to his leather and his thread, but repents too late. See the wretched women who left the needle, the spool, and the spindle, and became fortunetellers; they wrought spells with herbs and images.

As far as the facts of history are concerned, there is nothing especially problematic about this list. The thumbnail sketches of Michael Scot, Bonatti, and Asdente match for the most part other historical accounts, such as Villani's.[30] What is strange about this list is the voice that pronounces it. How does Virgil know about the "tricks" of Michael Scot, the Scottish translator of Aristotle who worked as court astrologer for Frederick II? Where can he have heard the nickname—Asdente—of the soothsayer-shoemaker Maestro Benvenuto? When did he learn to recognize Guido Bonatti, the roof-tiler-turned-astrologer who became famous in the second half of the thirteenth century and was still alive as late as 1296? If Virgil possesses, by God's grace, a thorough knowledge of modern Italian history, he shows it nowhere else in Dante's poem. In the hundreds of encounters that take place in Hell and Purgatory, there is no other case of Virgil naming (without prompting) a postclassical figure.[31] That Virgil can suddenly reel off a list of names and nicknames is, in the context of Dante's fiction, a troubling inconsistency.[32]

The deliberateness of this particular anomaly is confirmed through repetition. Even before Virgil names the modern seers, the Latin poet produces a strikingly up-to-date picture of the countryside around Mantua. As he traces Manto's passage across northern Italy, he casually mentions the castle Tiralli, built in the twelfth century by the counts of Venosta; he refers in passing to an island where the bishops of Brescia, Verona, and Trent share jurisdiction; and he praises the spanking new fortress built by the Scaligers in Peschiera—a fortress that was completed only years after Dante's putative journey through Hell.[33]

> Suso in Italia bella giace un laco,
>   a piè de l'Alpe che serra Lamagna
>   sovra Tiralli, c'ha nome Benaco.

Per mille fonti, credo, e più si bagna
    tra Garda e Val Camonica e Pennino
    de l'acqua che nel detto laco stagna.
Loco è nel mezzo là dove 'l trentino
    pastore e quel di Brescia e 'l veronese
    segnar poria, s'e' fesse quel cammino.
Siede Peschiera, bello e forte arnese
    da fronteggiar Bresciani e Bergamaschi,
    ove la riva 'ntorno più discese.

(Inf. 20.61–72)

Up in fair Italy, at the foot of the mountains that bound Germany above Tirol, lies a lake that is called Benaco. By a thousand springs, I think, and more, the region between Garda and Val Camonica and Pennino is bathed by the water that settles in that lake, and in the middle of it is a spot where the pastors of Trent, Brescia, and Verona, if they went that way, might give their blessing. Peschiera, a beautiful and strong fortress to confront the Brescians and Bergamese, sits where the surrounding shore is lowest.

At other points in the poem, Dante takes great pains to explain how it is that Virgil has acquired his fragmentary knowledge of modern history;[34] here, however, Dante gives us no clue how Virgil learned these remarkably specific details concerning the political, religious, and military organization of thirteenth-century Lombardy. This pattern continues to the very end of Virgil's lesson.

Fer la città sovra quell' ossa morte;
    e per colei che 'l loco prima elesse,
    Mantüa l'appellar sanz' altra sorte.
Già fuor le genti sue dentro più spesse,
    prima che la mattia da Casalodi
    da Pinamonte inganno ricevesse.
Però t'assenno che, se tu mai odi
    originar la mia terra altrimenti,
    la verità nulla menzogna frodi.

(Inf. 20.91–99)

They built a city over those dead bones, and for her who first chose the place they called it Mantua, without other augury. Once the people within it were more numerous, before the folly of Casalodi was tricked by Pinamonte. Therefore I charge you, if you ever hear a different origin given to my city, do not let such a lie defraud the truth.

Even as Dante voices his most aggressive defense of the *Inferno*'s historical veracity, he inserts an irrelevant historical detail—Pinamonte's betrayal of Count Casalodi in 1272—that threatens to upset the temporal conventions of his fiction.

The concentration of such numerous and various inconsistencies within *Inferno* 20 and *Purgatorio* 22 presents a serious challenge to those who would redeem miscitation by finding for it a corrective function. If one proposes to argue that Dante *deliberately* misrepresents Virgil's Manto to teach his readers a lesson, then one should be able to show that her misplacement is similarly deliberate and instructive. If one claims that the miscitations of *Inferno* 20 prove a point, then one should be able to find a purpose for the persistent flirtation with anachronism that takes place in the same canto. I do not imagine that such a challenge could not be met by a sufficiently ingenious interpreter. Wherever there are signs of a consciously wrought pattern, it is possible to argue for some subtle didactic intent, some understated program of readerly improvement or poetic self-discovery. Even a pattern of anomalies and contradictions can be construed as constructive and edifying. The important question is not whether we can (if we try hard enough) find a didactic function for Manto's misplacement or Dante's flirtation with anachronism, but whether that is the appropriate response. Should we allow our interpretive machine to become increasingly complex, or do we start again with a new set of assumptions?

I would urge the latter course, and I have my own suggestions about which assumptions are worth keeping and which can be rejected. I would accept with Hollander and Barolini that allegory is a critical concern in *Inferno* 20 and *Purgatorio* 22 and that Dante's relation to his pagan teachers is at issue in both cantos. But rather than emphasize the edifying logic of the cantos, I would stress their comic exuberance. What I find most surprising about *Inferno* 20 and *Purgatorio* 22 is the perverse economy of accidents—everything that goes wrong in these cantos seems to mirror some other structure or pattern: in the circle where false prophecy is punished, Dante allows Virgil to speak with a prophetic foreknowledge of Italian history; after redeeming Statius against all historical evidence, Dante has Virgil accidentally and inconsistently redeem Manto; in the very canto where Dante presents himself as an expert reader of the Latin tradition—someone who knows all of Virgil's *alta tragedìa* by heart—he commits the most astonishing citational blunders. Whenever the poet pretends to establish a rule or set a precedent, he simultaneously proceeds to violate it, deflect it, or parody it.

I would also give a different account of our readerly responsibilities. In most theories of corrective misreading, it is the reader's role to be impressed by Dante's display of interpretive authority and instructed by his edifying alterations. I would suggest that the reader of *Inferno* 20 and *Purgatorio* 22 is less Dante's student than his victim. Consider again the erudite references of *Inferno* 20. These allusions are, to a knowledgeable reader, potentially quite flattering. As Virgil congratulates Dante for his erudition, the erudite scholar may feel himself included. He may also know that Eurypylus is named only once in the *Aeneid*, he may also remember the passage in the *Pharsalia* where Arruns is named, he may also recognize the story of Mantua's origins. But if he smiles complacently at the breadth of his learning, if he feels drawn into the charmed circle of those who know the classics almost by heart, then he will have fallen into a trap; he will have mistaken an erudite joke on erudition for the real thing. That Dante is capable of playing such a dirty trick is clear from his correspondence with Giovanni del Virgilio. Promised a crown of laurels by the Bolognese humanist if he would only translate the *Comedy* from the "base common tongue" into Latin, Dante responds with a series of punishingly learned eclogues. Full of obscure references, vague allusions, and tortured syntactical evasions, these letters to Virgilio represent, as David Wallace observes, one of Dante's "cosmic jokes."[35]

The final alteration I would make concerns Dante's attitude toward his pagan predecessors. In many recent studies of "corrective misreading" and "creative misprision," Dante appears aggressive and ungrateful, an autocrat intent on claiming that he alone speaks the absolute truth. When we place the *Comedy*'s citational deformations in the context of other inconsistencies and anomalies—anomalies exclusively of Dante's creation—this aggressiveness is, I find, tempered.[36] Consider, from this perspective, the placement of Manto. Manto's position in Dante's invention is, we recall, ambiguous, but so too is the position of pagan poetry: sometimes it is damned as a fraud (*Inferno* 20), sometimes it is placed at the very edge of salvation (*Purgatorio* 22); sometimes pagan prophecy is treated as a false and dangerous delusion (*Inferno* 20), sometimes Dante suggests that pagan poetry *is* prophetic (*Purgatorio* 22). The technical problem of placing Manto thus opens into a much broader question: it invites us to contemplate the larger paradoxes subtended by Dante's project and his efforts to find the proper place for pagan poetry and prophecy.[37] It is worth remembering in this regard that Manto's name is linked both to the terms *mantica* and *negromante* and to the word for cloak—*manto*—the same word Dante uses in the *Convivio* to define the allegorical character of secular poetry:[38]

[The allegorical sense] è quello che si nasconde sotto 'l *manto* di queste favole, ed è una veritade ascosa sotto bella menzogna. (*Conv.* 2.1.3)[39]

[The allegorical sense] is the sense concealed under the *cloak* of these fables, and consists of a truth hidden under a beautiful lie.

Dante is not, I feel, asserting his right as Christian narrator to steal and distort at will; rather, he is admitting that his construction of a master narrative depends on masterful distortions. It is a comic deflation of an aggressive impulse rather than its expression, a gesture that is echoed in the works of many other medieval writers ranging from Petrarch to Chaucer.[40]

Chapter 4

Vanishing Acts

In a well-known address to the reader at the start of the *Paradiso*, Dante tries to dissuade part of his audience from continuing. He advises casual pleasure-seekers to turn back in their "piccioletta barca" unless they are prepared to lose their way on the broad, uncharted seas that lie ahead:

> O voi che siete in piccioletta barca,
> desiderosi d'ascoltar, seguiti
> dietro al mio legno che cantando varca,
> tornate a riveder li vostri liti:
> non vi mettete in pelago, ché forse,
> perdendo me, rimarreste smarriti.
>
> (*Par.* 2.1–6)

O you in your little bark, eager to hear, who have followed behind my ship that singing makes her way, turn back to see again your shores. Do not commit yourselves to the open sea, for you might perhaps lose me and remain lost.

Whether Dante is truly seeking to discourage us here from reading further or merely trying to stimulate our curiosity, he does alert us with this speech to a genuine problem: it is difficult, some might say impossible, to appreciate the *Paradiso* if one approaches it as a reprise of the *Inferno* and *Purgatorio*. Those qualities that draw us through the first two cantiche are notably absent from the last. In the *Paradiso*, Dante writes a poetry that, on the whole, appeals to the intellect rather than to emotion, memory, or a sense of adventure.

Many readers may privately lament this change in emphasis, but few would claim to find it incomprehensible. The poem's final austerity derives quite logically from its high aspirations: as Dante draws closer to God, he can no longer afford to dally with illusions, however powerful and appealing they may be. His business, in the end, is with Truth; and Truth, as we all know, is more taxing than fiction. If we want to keep reading with Dante, we have to be prepared to accept different kinds of compensation. Like the poet, we need, as readers, to mature.

This chapter is largely an attempt to resist growing up, or at least an attempt to resist the call to maturity as it is voiced so frequently in the critical literature about the *Paradiso*.[1] Its focus will be a series of scientific passages of a type peculiar to the final cantica, passages of such intimidating complexity that they seem better suited to a technical treatise on optics or geocentric astronomy than to a work of fiction. I shall argue that even these passages of lofty didacticism betray Dante's attachment to the types of anomaly and contradiction that surface in the earlier stages of the poem, and that I have been referring to collectively as error. Dante's final approach to God, I shall suggest, is as willfully erratic as any other segment of his poetic itinerary.

~~~~~

The connection between the *Paradiso*'s difficulty and its science is fairly straightforward: the sheer density of meteorological, optical, and geometrical allusion in the final cantica constitutes a serious impediment. In the first three cantos alone there are three conflicting theories about moonspots to struggle through, as well as an explanation of why fire rises, an exacting description of the laws of reflection from transparent surfaces, and an elaborate experiment with mirrors. After this daunting beginning, Dante immediately delves into other abstruse subjects: the causes of comets, the composition of the

Milky Way, the structure of rainbows, the precession of the equinoxes, and the arithmetic of the chessboard. By the *Paradiso*'s final canto, Dante has lectured on all four branches of the quadrivium, and he concludes, appropriately enough, by comparing himself to a frustrated geometer, a mathematician struggling to square the circle.

These scientific excursions present modern readers with a choice. We can read on quickly, glancing (perhaps) at a commentator's notes, or, if we are sufficiently patient and curious, we can set about drawing diagrams, poring over star-charts, and consulting Aristotle. The reward for such labors is commonly supposed to be a deepened appreciation for the rigor of Dante's thinking and the clarity of his explications. Moore speaks for the majority of scientifically inclined commentators when he praises Dante's expertise in matters astronomical. Dante, he notes, "may be 'hard' but he is seldom if ever obscure"; in science, as in all matters, his ideas are "as sharp in outline as if they were graven on a rock with a pen of iron."[2]

Though my goals are rather different from Moore's, I shall try to follow his advice: as I analyze several of the *Paradiso*'s more demanding scientific passages, I shall do my best to reveal their lapidary clarity. The first passage that I wish to consider is the dense lesson in geocentric astronomy inserted at the start of canto 10:

> Leva dunque, lettore, a l'alte rote
>   meco la vista, dritto a quella parte
>   dove l'un moto e l'altro si percuote;
> e lì comincia a vagheggiar ne l'arte
>   di quel maestro che dentro a sé l'ama,
>   tanto che mai da lei l'occhio non parte.
> Vedi come da indi si dirama
>   l'oblico cerchio che i pianeti porta,
>   per sodisfare al mondo che li chiama.
> Che se la strada lor non fosse torta,
>   molta virtù nel ciel sarebbe in vano,
>   e quasi ogne potenza qua giù morta;

e se dal dritto più o meno lontano
    fosse 'l partire, assai sarebbe manco
    e giù e sù de l'ordine mondano.
Or ti riman, lettor, sovra 'l tuo banco,
    dietro pensando a ciò che si preliba,
    s'esser vuoi lieto assai prima che stanco.
(*Par.* 10.7–24)

Lift then your sight with me, reader, to the lofty wheels, straight to that part where the one motion strikes the other; and amorously there begin to gaze upon that Master's art who within Himself so loves it that His eye never turns from it. See how from there the oblique circle that bears the planets branches off to satisfy the world that calls on them: and were their pathway not aslant, much virtue in the heavens would be vain and nearly every potency dead here below; and if it parted farther or less far from the straight course, much of the order of the world, both above and below, would be defective. Now remain, reader, upon your bench, reflecting on this of which you have a foretaste, if you would be glad far sooner than weary.

The general drift of this passage is clear even on cursory inspection; its subject is God's love of His creation, His plan for the cosmos, and the motion of the stars and planets. In its details, however, the lesson is far from transparent, and there are several questions a curious reader might want to ask: What are the "two motions" that Dante refers to? What is the "oblique circle"? And what is it exactly that we are supposed to see there in the sky where the two motions "strike one another"?

We can find answers by opening the *Convivio* to Dante's gloss on the canzone "Amore che ne la mente mi ragiona." In explicating this poem—a poem that says precious little about stars or planets—Dante provides a much plainer and much more systematic account of the various wheels, circles, and spheres that determine planetary motion. First, he points out that all celestial bodies are imbedded in a giant sphere that surrounds the earth and that turns on its axis once a day. On this vast sphere are two fixed points—the north and south celestial poles—and a rapidly turning central circle—the celestial equator:

Questo cielo si gira intorno a questo centro continuamente, sì come noi vedemo; ne la cui girazione conviene di necessitade essere due poli fermi, e uno cerchi equalmente distante da quelli, che massimamente giri. Di questi due poli, l'uno è manifesto quasi a tutta la terra discoperta,[3] cioè questo settentrionale; l'altro è quasi a tutta la discoperta terra celato, cioè lo meridionale. Lo cerchio che nel mezzo di questi s'intende, si è quella parte del cielo sotto la quale si gira lo sole, quando va con l'Ariete e con la Libra. (*Conv.* 3.5.8)

These heavens revolve unceasingly around this center, as we ourselves observe; in this revolution there must necessarily be two fixed poles and a circle equidistant from them that revolves with the greatest speed. Of these two poles, one, this northern pole, is observable to almost all the uncovered earth; the other, southern, pole is hidden to almost all the uncovered earth. The circle that is understood to be midway between these poles is that part of the heavens under which the sun revolves when it is in the constellations of the Ram and the Scales.

Later in the same chapter, Dante describes a second sphere lodged concentrically within the first. Unlike the outer sphere, which, when it rotates, moves every celestial body, the inner sphere is specifically associated with the sun. It turns in the opposite direction from that of the outer sphere and at a slight angle. The equator of the smaller sphere (the ecliptic) thus cuts ("sega") the equator of the larger sphere (the celestial equator) at two points—these, Dante explains, are the "first points" in Aries and Libra, the signs[4] in which the sun is located at spring and fall equinox respectively:

Il cielo del sole si rivolge da occidente in oriente, non dirittamente contra lo movimento diurno, cioè del die e de la notte, ma tortamente contra quello; sì che 'l suo mezzo cerchio che equalmente è 'n tra li suoi poli, nel quale è lo corpo del sole, sega in due parti opposite lo cerchio de li due primi poli, cioè nel principio de l'Ariete e nel principio de la Libra. (*Conv.* 3.5.13)

The heaven of the Sun revolves from west to east tracing a path not directly contrary to that followed by the daily movement (that is, the movement of day and night), but obliquely contrary to it, so that its

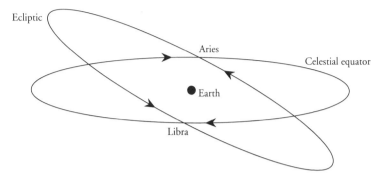

Figure 7. The ecliptic and the celestial equator (*Paradiso* 10).

equator (where the body of the sun is located), lying equidistant from its poles, intersects the circle between the first two poles [the celestial equator] at two opposite points, that is, at the beginning of the Ram and at the beginning of the Scales.

With the help of these two passages, we can now identify most of the obscure terms employed in *Paradiso* 10.7–24.[5] The two motions Dante points out to the reader—"l'un moto e l'altro"—are the contrary motions of the two spheres that carry the stars and the sun; the point where those motions strike one another—"quella parte / dove l'un moto e l'altro si percuote"—is the point where the ecliptic cuts across the celestial equator. There are two such intersections. One is located in Aries, the other in Libra. It is from each of these points that the "twisted path" of the ecliptic branches away from the celestial equator (see Figure 7 and compare with Figures 8 and 9).[6]

Still unclear, however, is the poet's intense interest in these astronomical figures. Why is it that Dante directs our attention specifically to the crossing point of the "two motions"? Why is it that God loves this point so much that "da lei l'occhio non parte?" According to John Freccero, the answer lies with Plato, or, more accurately, with the commentaries on Plato's *Timaeus* passed down from Chalcidius to medieval readers.[7] In this cosmological tradition, the crossing point of the two motions is no less than the blueprint and foundation of the entire

Figure 8. Armillary sphere from *Epytoma in Almagestum Ptolemaei* (1496). Courtesy of Chapin Library, Williams College.

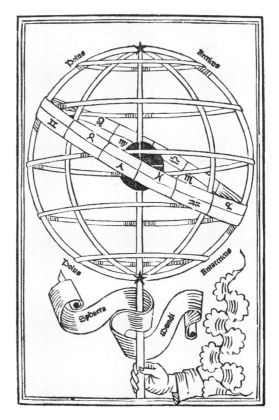

Figure 9. Armillary sphere from *Sphericum Opusculum* (1485). Courtesy of Chapin Library, Williams College.

physical universe. The Demiurge whom Plato credits with bringing the cosmos into being begins his work by molding the bundled fabric of the world soul into a shape resembling the Greek letter *chi*—X. He then folds the ends of this X in upon themselves to form two circles and sets these circles in motion. One circle (the circle of the same, that is, the celestial equator) eventually carries the sun and stars in their diurnal motion from east to west. The other circle (the circle of the different, that is, the ecliptic) will carry the sun in a much slower zodiacal motion from west to east.

This whole fabric [of the world soul], then, he split lengthwise into two halves; and making the two cross one another at their centers in the form of the letter X, he bent each round into a circle and joined it up, making each meet itself and the other at a point opposite to that where they had been brought into contact. He then comprehended them in the motion that is carried round uniformly in the same place, and made the one the outer, the other the inner circle. The outer movement he named the movement of the Same [the diurnal rotation of the entire celestial sphere]; the inner, the movement of the Different [the contrary rotation of the planetary spheres].[8]

At least as important to Dante as the original myth is the use made of it by Christian exegetes. In the eyes of Abelard and Guillame di Conche, the Greek *chi* that Plato describes is actually a cross; the Platonic allegory is, they claim, really a Christological prophecy.[9] Writing earlier in this century, Hugo Rahner sympathetically summarizes the cosmic vision of these medieval Christians:

God, who from the beginning of time has secretly looked upon the coming cross of his Son, has stamped the pattern of that cross on the foundation of the world, has made it the ground-plan in the building of the universe. The two great circles of the heavens, the equator and the ecliptic which, by intersecting each other, form a sort of recumbent chi and about which the whole dome of the starry heavens swings in a wondrous rhythm, become for the Christian eye a heavenly cross.[10]

Placing Dante's astronomical lesson within this tradition enables us to interpret it much more precisely. Though Dante may only refer to the celestial cross explicitly in the third terzina, we can see that it is already the implicit subject of the first lines describing God's creation of the universe:

> Guardando nel suo Figlio con l'Amore
> che l'uno e l'altro etternalmente spira,
> lo primo e ineffabile Valore
> quanto per mento e per loco si gira
> con tant'ordine fé ch'esser non puote
> sanza gustar di lui chi ciò rimira.
> (*Par.* 10.1–6)

Looking upon His Son with the love which the One and the Other eternally breathe forth, the primal and ineffable Power made everything that revolves through the mind or through space with such order that he who contemplates it cannot but taste of Him.

The phrase "tant'ordine" does not refer to some vague, abstract concept of cosmic order; it expressly refers to the order that governs the turning of the spheres, the Platonic motion of the Same and the Different. Since this twofold motion sketches a cross in the heavens, all contemplation of heavenly motion is implicitly Christological; it is impossible to contemplate the movements of the stars and planets "sanza gustar di lui." The *passato remoto* "fé" in line 5 alludes to the principal cosmogonic act, the formation of the celestial cross, and this explains the otherwise puzzling "dunque" of line 7: having just revised the creation myth of the *Timaeus* and having found a Christian function for Plato's "*chi* in the sky," Dante invites us to gaze up into the heavens and see it for ourselves: "Leva *dunque*, lettore, a l'alte rote / meco la vista."

Canto 10 is a logical place for Dante to teach us this lesson for two reasons. First, the number 10 (X) is itself a symbol of the Cross; second, canto 10 describes the sphere of the sun. Like the celestial cross, the sun is a standard symbol for Christ: it is a homiletic commonplace to refer to Christ as the "Sun of Righteousness" (*Sol Iustitiae*); the sun's "suffering" at sunset on Good Friday and its "resurrection" on Easter morning are, moreover, standard elements of the liturgy.[11] Beatrice draws upon this traditional symbolism when she calls upon Dante in canto 10 to offer thanks to God, whom she suggestively titles "Sol de li angeli":

> E Bëatrice cominciò: "Ringrazia,
> ringrazia il Sol de li angeli, ch'a questo
> sensibil t'ha levato per sua grazia."
> (*Par.* 10.52–54)

And Beatrice began, "Give thanks, give thanks to the Sun of the Angels who of His grace has raised you to this visible one."

Just as it is the sun, in the medieval worldview, that illuminates the stars, so it is God, the invisible sun, whose spiritual light reflects onto the earth from starlike angels.

The previous paragraphs demonstrate, I hope, the potential benefits of Moore's approach to the *Paradiso*'s "hard" science: by attempting to clarify difficult points in the astronomical lesson, we have come to better appreciate the passage's lofty tone and subject matter; references that might have seemed vague and obscure at first glance turn out to be densely, but precisely, allusive. There is, however, one aspect of the lesson that Moore's approach does not adequately address: its peculiar insistence on sight. The first 27 lines of canto 10 differ from the rest of the *Paradiso* insofar as their subject is not the imaginary space envisaged by the poet, but the real heavens turning about the reader's head. Dante asks us to look up from our books toward the skies and enforces this shift in perspective through a series of strict imperatives: "*Leva* . . . la vista, dritto a quella parte . . ."; "lì *comincia* a vagheggiar . . ."; "*Vedi* come da indi si dirama. . . ." Dante's instructions are clear and insistent; we are to lift our eyes, see, and enjoy. Even God is shown by Dante engaged in the act of looking; He is so enamored of the cosmic X that "His eye never leaves it" ("da lei l'occhio non parte"). Given such instructions, one might conclude that there must be something wonderful to see there where the two bands cross one another—some unusually bright star or constellation. There is, however, *nothing to see*. The bands of the ecliptic and equator are themselves invisible, and they intersect in a dim, uninteresting section of the night sky. For all Dante's talk, the "*chi* in the sky" is only imaginary, and the only place it can actually be observed is on a mechanical model of the heavens, an armillary sphere, astrolabe, or orrery constructed by an astronomer.

Assigning a didactic function to this surprise would not, of course, be difficult. Dante's insistence that we try to see what cannot be seen reinforces the distinction between spiritual and physical vision that is so central to the philosophical and religious discourse of the *Paradiso*; our surprise reminds us of the essential difference between the "Sol de li angeli" and the merely "visible" sun (*sol sensibil*) that illuminates the stars. But the fact that we can moralize our surprise should not prevent us from acknowledging the lesson's peculiar structure. The process of comprehending what Dante is doing in *Paradiso* 10 involves a moment of genuine uncertainty about what we can and cannot hope to visualize in the poem. As a teacher, Dante offers instructions that, if taken literally, lead the student toward a basic misunderstanding.

For reasons that will become clear later in this chapter, I believe this moment of uncertainty to be as significant as any other element in the lesson. I would even suggest that it is precisely the moment of readerly doubt and confusion that links this lesson to the *Paradiso*'s other scientific passages. For now, however, I would prefer to move on to another difficult moment: the description of balanced planets that launches canto 29.

> Quando ambedue li figli di Latona,
>   coperti del Montone e de la Libra,
>   fanno de l'orizzonte insieme zona,
> quant' è dal punto che 'l cenìt inlibra
>   infin che l'uno e l'altro da quel cinto,
>   cambiando l'emisperio, si dilibra,
> tanto, col volto di riso dipinto,
>   si tacque Beatrice, riguardando
>   fiso nel punto che m'avea vinto.
>
> (*Par.* 29.1–9)

When the two children of Latona, covered by the Ram and by the Scales, make the horizon their belt at one same moment, as long as from the instant when the zenith holds them balanced till the one and the other, changing hemispheres, are unbalanced from that belt, for so long, her face illumined with a smile, was Beatrice silent, looking fixedly at the point that had overcome me.

Like the lesson of canto 10, this passage is a striking instance of intricate, technically demanding astronomy. In order to discover the duration of Beatrice's smiling silence, Dante asks his readers to undertake the construction of a complex cosmic clock—an assemblage of planets, horizons, and hemispheres that no reader (no matter how skilled and experienced) could possibly comprehend on a single reading. The first step is sorting out the pieces that go into the clock's construction:

li figli di Latona—the sun and moon;
Montone and *Libra*—the zodiacal signs corresponding to the
    sun's position at spring and fall equinox;
orizzonte—the horizon of an earthbound observer watching
    the balancing act;
cenìt—zenith—the point directly over the observer's head;
emisperio—the half-sphere determined by the observer's po-
    sition.

Next we need to work out how these pieces fit together. Since the sun and moon "fanno de l'orizzonte insieme zona" and since the zenith acts to "balance" them ("inlibra"), they must be in the process of rising and setting on opposite horizons. Their arrangement is typically represented using a diagram such as that shown in Figure 10: as one planet rises above the horizon, the other settles beneath it. We are asked to imagine a full moon rising in the light of a setting sun, or, alternatively, a full moon setting opposite a rising sun. In addition to situating the planets on the horizon, Dante also situates them in the zodiacal signs of Aries and Libra. This extra information determines the date of the balancing act—fall or spring equinox—and connects this image to the astronomical lesson of canto 10. The sun and moon are located at each of the two "crosses" where the celestial equator intersects the ecliptic (see Figure 11).

Having visualized the positions of the balanced planets, we can now calculate the duration of their equilibrium and, as a consequence, the duration of Beatrice's silent smile. Here two different schools of interpretation exist. According to Manfred Porena and his followers, the balancing act lasts as long as it takes for the sun and moon to free themselves entirely from the belt of the horizon—a period Porena claims should last

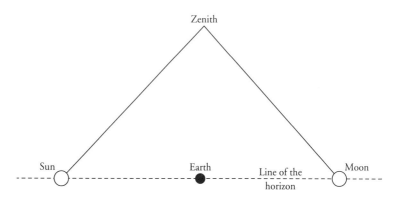

Figure 10. Celestial clockwork (1) (*Paradiso 29*).

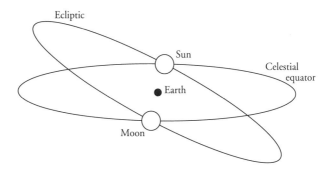

Figure 11. Celestial clockwork (2) (*Paradiso 29*).

"about a minute."[12] According to another group of readers, the balancing act lasts only as long as the two planets remain exactly opposite one another—a period that is of infinitesimal duration.[13] Though the arguments proposed by both sides are intriguing, the most revealing aspect of the debate is, arguably, its very existence. Dante has constructed such a complicated image that the simple, straightforward task of measuring time becomes a matter for scholarly dispute. The turn to astronomical metaphor may lend grandeur to the scene, but it comes at the cost of poetic immediacy; following the poem's narrative and visualizing its imagery become increasingly frustrating and difficult.

Nor do such difficulties disperse as we become more familiar with Dante's astronomical method. For as several readers (including Porena) have noted, there is something even more puzzling about Dante's precise instructions than their complexity. Consider again Figures 10 and 11, this time taking account of the earth's position within each diagram. What you should notice is that the earth is exactly collinear with the sun and the moon. This precise arrangement of the three celestial bodies produces the unexpected effect of rendering the complex clockwork invisible. It would be impossible for an earthbound observer to gauge the duration of the balancing act because the alignment that engenders a perfect planetary balance also engenders a perfect lunar eclipse.[14]

This eclipse is not easily accommodated in traditional accounts of Dante's science. According to critics like Moore and Nardi, the movement toward comprehension should be steady and direct. With every new diagram, difficulties should drop away. In canto 29 the reverse happens. We have a harder time seeing clearly the more intently we stare. Our situation is not so very different from that of the overexcited eclipse-watcher whom Dante imagines gradually losing his sight and to whom the poet compares himself in *Paradiso* 25. This loss of sight is, furthermore, critical to understanding the canto. For if our discovery of the eclipse prevents us from "seeing" the clockwork in action, that moment of blindness also makes possible new insights. One immediately notices that vision is a major topic in canto 29, that two visionary blindings bracket the canto, and that eclipse is one of its central themes. In a long and violent harangue, Beatrice attacks those theologians who would find a purely physical cause for the solar eclipse that, according to Luke, accompanied Christ's crucifixion:[15]

> Per apparer ciascun s'ingegna e face
>   sue invenzioni; e quelle son trascorse
>   da' predicanti e 'l Vangelio si tace.
> Un dice che la luna si ritorse
>   ne la passion di Cristo e s'interpuose,
>   per che 'l lume del sol giù non si porse;

> e mente, ché la luce si nascose
>   da sé: però a li Spani e a l'Indi
>   come a' Giudei tale eclissi rispuose.
> Non ha Fiorenza tanti Lapi e Bindi
>   quante sì fatte favole per anno
>   in pergamo si gridan quinci e quindi.
>
>   *(Par.* 29.94–105)

Each one strives for display and makes his own inventions, and these
are treated by the preachers, and the Gospel is silent. One says that
at Christ's passion the moon turned back and interposed itself, so that
the light of the sun did not reach below—and he lies, for the light
itself hid itself, so that this eclipse took place for the Spaniards and
the Indians, as well as for the Jews. Florence has not so many Lapos
and Bindos as fables such as these that are shouted the year long from
the pulpits on every side.

The *favola* Beatrice rebukes here with such vehemence de-
pends on the same essential mechanism that produces the
eclipse of Dante's astronomical clock. In one case it is the body
of the earth that blocks the sun's light, in the other case it is the
body of the moon. This symmetry is, I believe, more than just
a quirky coincidence; it is an invitation to the reader to take a
second, closer look at the tantalizingly precise alignment of the
planets described at the start of the canto.

Rather than continuing to outline ways of making sense of
this eclipse (there are many possibilities),[16] I want to shift at-
tention to a third scientific passage—the mirror experiment
recounted by Beatrice in canto 2:

> Tre specchi prenderai; e i due rimovi
>   da te d'un modo, e l'altro, più rimosso,
>   tr'ambo li primi li occhi tuoi ritrovi.
> Rivolto ad essi, fa che dopo il dosso
>   ti stea un lume che i tre specchi accenda
>   e torni a te da tutti ripercosso.
> Ben che nel quanto tanto non si stenda
>   la vista più lontana, lì vedrai
>   come convien ch'igualmente risplenda.
>
>   *(Par.* 2.97–105)

You shall take three mirrors, and set two of them equally remote from you, and let the other, even more remote, meet your eyes between the first two. Turning toward them, cause a light to be placed behind your back which may shine in the three mirrors and return to you reflected from all three. Although the more distant image may not seem as large as the others, you will see that it shines with equal brightness.

The first thing to notice about this passage is its precision. As Beatrice outlines the experiment, she tells Dante exactly where to place the mirrors and the lamp and exactly where he should stand (see Figures 12–14). Beatrice is equally explicit about what Dante should see when he gazes into the various mirrors: first, he should note that the lamp appears smaller when viewed in the more distant mirror ("nel quanto tanto non si stenda / la vista più lontana"), and second, he should observe that all three of the reflected images display the same apparent brilliance ("lì vedrai / come convien ch'igualmente risplenda"). The first claim is not at all surprising;[17] our intuition suggests that as a mirror is moved farther away from an observer, so objects viewed in that mirror will appear smaller. The important, and for most readers unexpected, claim involves the images' comparative luminosity. Until we perform the experiment we might well suppose that the more distant image of the lamp would appear less bright than the closer image. The purpose of the experiment is to correct this false assumption and to demonstrate by direct observation that the brightness of a reflected image is independent of the distance between observer and mirror.

There is considerable confusion in the commentary tradition over the validity of this assertion. Singleton, Grandgent, and other commentators have strongly implied that Dante's claim stems from an observational error: "If, as seems likely, Dante had actually performed this experiment, he must have done so under such conditions that, *to his eye*, his conclusion was shown to be correct" (emphasis mine).[18] Yet on a theoretical level, at least, the experiment is perfectly valid. An observer comparing the brightness of images produced by differently positioned mirrors is effectively comparing the bright-

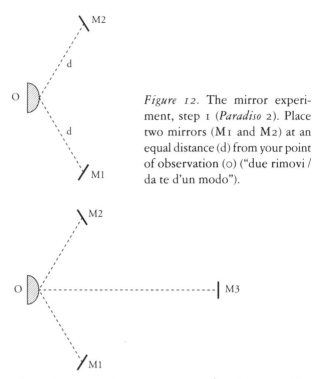

Figure 12. The mirror experiment, step 1 (*Paradiso* 2). Place two mirrors (M1 and M2) at an equal distance (d) from your point of observation (o) ("due rimovi / da te d'un modo").

Figure 13. The mirror experiment, step 2 (*Paradiso* 2). Place a third mirror (M3) directly between M1 and M2, but at a greater distance (D) from yourself ("l'altro, piu rimosso, / tr'ambo li primi li occhi tuoi ritrovi").

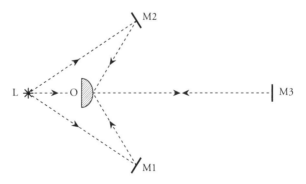

Figure 14. The mirror experiment, step 3 (*Paradiso* 2). Place a lamp (L) behind your back so that it will illuminate all three mirrors ("fa che dopo il dosso / ti stea un lume che i tre specchi accenda / e torni a te da tutti ripercosso").

ness of identical lamps placed at different distances from the eye. The perceived luminosity of a lamp or, for that matter, any bright object does *not* depend on the distance between the source of light and the observer. Although less light reaches the eye from a distant light source, the image of that distant source formed on the retina is correspondingly smaller. These two effects exactly balance each other out.[19]

The mirror experiment is itself imbedded in a much larger scientific discussion. It enters the poem as a single section in a complicated (indeed, to some readers, baffling) discussion of moonspots, those dark patches on the lunar surface that we recognize as the "man in the moon." This well-known phenomenon vexed medieval cosmologists because it seemed to belie the neat distinction between terrestrial flux and celestial perfection: the moon, a heavenly body, seemed tainted—the spots seemed evidence that even the celestial spheres were subject to damage and decay.[20] The experiment sheds some light on this puzzle because it serves as a miniature model of the heavens: the light spreading from the lamp toward the mirrors represents the sun's light spreading toward the moon; the various mirrors represent the moon's uneven surface; and the observer represents an earthbound spectator. If the intensity of reflected light appears to differ from mirror to mirror, then the unevenness of the moon's surface could conceivably account for the existence of dark and bright patches. (The dim, distant mirrors would correspond to the dark spots on the moon's surface, while the closer, brighter mirrors would correspond to the moon's more luminous regions.) Since all the mirrors produce equally brilliant reflections, Beatrice concludes that this *cannot* be the correct explanation of why the moon's surface appears spotted. The experiment does not identify the correct cause of moonspots, but it does lay one tempting hypothesis to rest—a hypothesis that Dante had earlier championed in the *Convivio*.[21]

On scientific grounds alone, there is much to praise in the mirror experiment. Few of Dante's contemporaries sought to measure the comparative brightness of distant light sources, and when they did offer theories and predictions, they were often wrong. On this point stumbled Alhazen, Grosseteste, and Bacon, all of whom asserted (mistakenly) that distant objects necessarily appear less bright than closer ones.[22] Dante's claim that image intensity is independent of distance is thus surprisingly original as well as correct.[23] No less innovative is the conceptual frame of the experiment. In using lamps and mirrors to model the behavior of the sun and the moon, Dante is working against a scientific tradition that tended to draw sharp distinctions between terrestrial and celestial phenomena—a tradition that was quite strong even in the days of Galileo.

Yet for all of the experiment's acuity and sophistication, it does have one drawback. Though its conclusion is valid, it is, as described by Beatrice, unperformable.[24] The problem with her instructions is essentially geometrical and becomes apparent as soon as one actually tries to perform the experiment using a real lamp and real mirrors. Since the observer stands directly between the lamp and the distant mirror, the light spreading from the lamp will be blocked by his or her body before it reaches that mirror. It will be impossible for the experimenter to compare the intensity of the various reflections because only the closer mirrors will be illuminated. Describing the problem in astronomical terms, one might say that the observer's opaque body will act to "eclipse" the lamp's moon.

Critics have been reticent about this difficulty. Indeed, the only published acknowledgments of the problem that I have located represent efforts to push it out of sight. One instance is Moore's analysis of the experiment in *Studies in Dante*.[25] Moore never points out to his readers the error in the experiment's design, yet he betrays his awareness of it by introducing a series of corrective adjustments (see Figure 15). In Moore's version, the two closer mirrors (M1 and M2) are *not* an equal distance from the lamp, the distant mirror (M3) is *not* situated directly between the two closer mirrors, and the lamp (L) is *not*

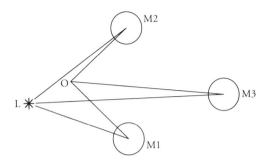

Figure 15. Moore's representation of the mirror experiment (*Paradiso* 2). Redrawn from Moore, *Studies in Dante.*

positioned behind the observer's back. This asymmetric version clearly does not match Dante's description, but it has the advantage of actually working; by breaking the experiment's perfect symmetry, Moore quietly solves the problem that symmetry creates. A more open admission of the problem is to be found in Bosco and Reggio's gloss on the phrase "dopo il dosso":

dopo il dosso—dietro le spalle; è sottinteso *naturalmente* che il dosso non deve coprire la fonte luminosa, perché altrimenti gli specchi non potrebbe rifleterne la luce.[26]

behind your back—It is understood, *of course*, that one shouldn't cover the luminous source with one's back, because otherwise the mirrors will not be able to reflect the light.

Here again the critics' recognition of the experiment's flaw triggers an immediate effort to diminish it. From the phrasing of the note, Bosco and Reggio make it quite clear that they view the misalignment of the mirrors as a problem barely worthy of their attention. Only a fool, they suggest, would be seriously troubled by Dante's instructions; if there appears to be an error in the experiment's design it will, *naturalmente*, have a solution.

What Bosco, Reggio, and Moore don't point out is that Dante

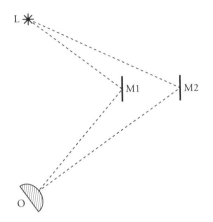

Figure 16. An alternative version of the mirror experiment (*Paradiso* 2).

has gone to a great deal of trouble to engineer the error they endeavor to diminish. To prove his theory about reflected light, Dante need employ only two mirrors (not three), and those mirrors can be positioned in a variety of ways; Figure 16 shows a simple, functional version, and there are a great many other possibilities.[27] There is no reason for the experiment to fail unless the experimenter makes the mistake of standing between the lamp and the mirror. This is a very unlikely blunder, yet Dante compels us to make it. His needlessly elaborate arrangement of the mirrors and his careful step-by-step instructions force us into a position where we will find our all-too-solid bodies getting in the way.

Of the scientific passages analyzed so far, Dante's detailed description of an unperformable experiment is, to my mind, the most surprising. Although we can, as always, devise a didactic function for our frustration, it is hard to argue that any moral—no matter how illuminating or instructive—outweighs our shock at being deceived. Beatrice's scholastic pose, her confident pronouncements, and her defense of experiment ("esperïenza") all seem calculated to lead us astray:[28]

Da questa instanza può deliberarti

esperïenza, *se già mai la provi,*
ch'esser suol fonte ai rivi di vostr' arti.
(*Par.* 2.94–96)

From this objection, experiment, which is wont to be the fountain to the stream of your arts, may deliver you, *if ever you try it.*

Beatrice describes the experiment as if it were primarily about optics, but if we take Beatrice's advice to heart, if we actually go to the trouble of arranging the mirrors and the lamp, we learn more about ourselves than we do about the behavior of light and polished surfaces. What we discover in the experiment is our own corporeality.

~

All three of the scientific excursuses reviewed in this chapter could be described as vanishing acts: in each case Dante lures us with a show of scientific precision into trying to visualize the invisible. What I find most intriguing about these vanishing acts—and what I have tried to foreground in my analysis—is their extreme subtlety. It is only after investing considerable energy in interpreting these dense scientific passages that we can begin to recognize how difficult and odd they really are.[29] And yet, if the vanishing acts are exceptionally subtle in their execution, they are not so strange or foreign that we cannot find a place for them in the larger development of the *Paradiso.* Frustration, blindness, and surprise are, in a very immediate way, present throughout the final cantica and are experienced no less by the traveler than by the reader. In the sphere of Mercury, Justinian's *ombra* blazes so brightly that Dante loses sight of his human form. In the sphere of the sun, the gyrating rings of theologians erase themselves from Dante's vision with a sudden explosion of light. At the edge of the Empyrean, Dante looks for the form of John's body, and, like an eclipse-watcher, finds himself blinded for more than half a canto:

Qual è colui ch'adocchia e s'argomenta
di vedere eclissar lo sole un poco,
che, per veder, non vedente diventa;

tal mi fec' io a quell' ultimo foco
mentre che detto fu: "Perché t'abbagli
per veder cosa che qui non ha loco?"
(*Par.* 25.118–23)

As he who gazes and strains to see the sun a little eclipsed, and who through seeing becomes sightless, so did I become gazing at that last fire, till it was said, "Why do you dazzle yourself in order to see that which has here no place?"

These blindings are not casual events; they structure the traveler's ascent just as surely as do his moments of ecstatic insight. If Dante could complete his journey to God with his eyes always open, it would suggest a proximity and accessibility that run counter to his aims. The *Paradiso* is not so much about seeing as it is about seeing limitations.

That science, or at least the rhetoric of science, should be incorporated into this project makes perfect sense. Scientific language suggests accuracy, lucidity, and precision; it is a language aimed at placing the physical world under the mastery of reason. In a poem devoted to mapping the limits of human comprehension, such complacent expectations about the clarity of science present an ideal target. Consider, for example, Dante's use of technical, astronomical terminology at the start of canto 13:

Imagini, chi bene intender cupe
quel ch'i' or vidi—e ritenga l'image,
mentre ch'io dico, come ferma rupe—,
quindici stelle che 'n diverse plage
lo cielo avvivan di tanto sereno
che soperchia de l'aere ogne compage;
imagini quel carro a cu' il seno
basta del nostro cielo e notte e giorno,
sì ch'al volger del temo non vien meno;
imagini la bocca di quel corno
che si comincia in punta de lo stelo
a cui la prima rota va dintorno,
aver fatto di sé due segni in cielo,

qual fece la figliuola di Minoi
allora che sentì di morte il gelo;
e l'un ne l'altro aver li raggi suoi,
e amendue girarsi per maniera,
che l'uno andasse al primo e l'altro al poi;
e avrà quasi l'ombra de la vera
costellazione e de la doppia danza
che circulava il punto dov'io era.
(Par. 13.1–21)

Let him imagine, who would rightly grasp what I now beheld (and while I speak, let him hold the image firm as a rock), fifteen stars which in different regions vivify the heaven with such great brightness that it overcomes every thickness of the air; let him imagine that Wain for which the bosom of our heaven suffices night and day so that with the turning of the pole it does not disappear; let him imagine the mouth of that Horn which begins at the end of the axle on which the first wheel revolves—all to have made of themselves two signs in the heavens like that which the daughter of Minos made when she felt the chill of death; and one to have its rays within the other, and both to revolve in such manner that one should go first and the other after; and he will have as it were a shadow of the true constellation, and of the double dance which was circling round the point where I was.

Like the other scientific passages analyzed, this address to the well-intended reader—the reader who desires to "bene intender"—creates a scene through a series of well-defined stages. First this reader is encouraged to "imagine" the fifteen stars of the Northern Hemisphere that, according to Ptolemy's catalogue, are of the first magnitude in brightness. Next he is told to "imagine" the seven conspicuous stars of the Great Dipper ("quel carro"). Then he is asked to "imagine" the two second-magnitude stars that lie in the mouth of the Little Dipper ("quel corno"). Having gathered together these 24 stars from diverse constellations, the reader is finally called upon to reconstellate them—he is instructed to make of these bright stars a more resplendent (and more complex) version of the circular constellation known to astronomers as "Ariadne's crown."

Though Dante's instructions to the reader occupy a full seven terzine, few are likely to mistake the passage for a serious effort at representing the circles of luminous theologians clearly and distinctly. The elaborate astronomical allusions do not help us to see the spiraling rings; rather, they make the task more difficult—and more exciting. Gathering and rearranging stars is an exercise of the imagination that leads nowhere in particular but that, in its splendid impracticality, may (or may not) produce pleasure. Dante can afford to allow himself this pause, this digression into an aimless aesthetic space, because in paradise nothing more can be hoped for from his poetry. The reader may try his best to "grasp" ("ritenga") the poet's vision, but in the end he will have no more than a "shadow" of that transcendent reality: "quasi l'ombra de la vera / costellazione."[30] The excesses and indirection of the pseudoscientific procedure indicate a critical gap between the poet's language and his ineffable subject matter.

That there is a connection between the impossible project of the *Paradiso* and the poem's playful pyrotechnics is apparent at a number of other critical junctures. One could cite in this regard moments of high whimsy like the marvelous but essentially pointless flapping of the eagle in the sphere of Jupiter.[31] Or one could point to the similes and metaphors that ostensibly show us Paradise, yet actually interfere with our efforts to visualize the lightscape—similes involving such flamboyant absurdities as inverted flaming snowfalls and planetlike birds exchanging luminous plumage.[32] But the connection is perhaps most clear in the bemusement that the discovery of error provokes among the blessed. After Beatrice is asked by Dante to explain the causes of moonspots, the first thing she does is smile ("sorrise"). When Gregory discovers that he had confused in his writings the order of the angelic hierarchy—jumbled the positions of the Thrones, Powers, Principalities, and Dominations—he does not groan with embarrassment, but rather smiles to himself ("di sé medesmo rise," 28.135). Dante, gazing back at the once-great earth, smiles ("sorridere") to discover its "vil sembiante" (*Par.* 22.135).[33] These "post-palinodic" smiles mark out, as Rachel Jacoff has observed, a new stage in the poem.[34] In the *Paradiso*, the poet enters a region where the discovery of error resolves toward laughter rather than pathos or corrosive irony, where the foreknowledge of failure is no longer distressful but liberating. As the troubadour Folco explains to Dante, "Non però qui si pente, ma si ride" (Here one does not repent, one smiles). What the poet reaches, in the end, is the privilege of merging error with play.[35]

I could end my analysis of the vanishing acts at this point with some degree of satisfaction. The notion that Dante's elaborate arrangements of mirrors and planets are ultimately aesthetic rather than didactic is one that I find quite congenial. I am not going to break off here, however, because there is one aspect of the vanishing acts that I feel still needs to be addressed: though I have presented the invisible cross, the self-eclipsing clockwork, and the unperformable experiment as distinct moments, they are, in fact, intimately associated. Each is part of a carefully executed pattern.

The clearest sign of this pattern is the consistent recurrence of the word *eclisso*. Appearing only five times in the entire *Comedy*, *eclisso* appears in each of the three cantos we have been analyzing. In canto 2, Beatrice explains that moonspots cannot be produced by holes in the moon because, if that were the case, those holes would allow light to shine through during every solar eclipse:

> Se 'l primo fosse, fora manifesto
>   ne l'*eclissi* del sol, per trasparere
>   lo lume come in altro raro ingesto.
> Questo non è.
>
> (*Par.* 2.79–82)

If the first were the case, this would be manifest in the *eclipse* of the sun, by the shining through of the light, as it does when it is poured upon any rare matter. This is not so.

In *Paradiso* 10, eclipse functions as a metaphor for describing a moment of ecstatic insight and oblivion. After Beatrice calls on Dante to thank the "Sol de li angeli," the poet finds his vision of Beatrice momentarily "eclipsed" by God:

> Cor di mortal non fu mai sì digesto
> a divozione e a rendersi a Dio
> con tutto 'l suo gradir cotanto presto,
> come a quelle parole mi fec' io;
> e sì tutto 'l mio amore in lui si mise,
> che Beatrice *eclissò* ne l'oblio.
>
> (*Par.* 10.55–60)

Never was mortal heart so disposed to devotion and so ready, with all its gratitude, to give itself to God, as I became at those words. And all my love was so set on Him that it *eclipsed* Beatrice in oblivion.

I have already cited the passage in canto 29 where the term *eclisso* is used. When Beatrice vilifies theologians for their vain speculations, she centers her attack on their attempts to explain, in physical terms, the miraculous darkness—eclipse—that accompanied Christ's suffering on the Cross.

A second, more elusive link among the cantos is the recurrent motif of the cross. At the start of *Paradiso* 10, Dante focuses our attention on the celestial cross in Aries, then proceeds to transfix the sun at its center.[36] In *Paradiso* 29, Dante repeats this scene of astronomical crucifixion and also alludes to Christ's crucifixion. In canto 2, Dante builds a cross of mirrors at whose center an observer is "crucified" (see Figure 14). This is a subtle, but nonetheless suggestive, pattern. Because it is recorded in Luke that the sun darkened at the moment of Christ's passion, eclipse became a dominant theme in representations and discussions of the Crucifixion during the Middle Ages. Aquinas devotes an entire section of his commentary on Luke 23 to postulating possible causes for the solar eclipse.[37] Cecco D'Ascoli and Sacrobosco conclude their astronomical treatises by speculating on the Crucifixion eclipse's mystical significance.[38] Abelard, in his *Hymnarius paraclitensis*, extends the traditional association between Christ and the sun by likening the sun's "suffering" in eclipse to the "True Sun's" suffering on the Cross: "Cum crucem sustinens Sol Versus patitur / Sol insensibilis illi compatitur."[39] The Crucifixion scenes produced by medieval illuminators and enamel workers commonly include eclipsed suns and moons, occasionally even giving the suffering of the planets precedence over the suffering of Mary and the angels.[40] Dante's personal interest in the Crucifixion eclipse is manifest at several points. The eclipse is an explicit topic in *Paradiso* 29 and is also openly discussed in *Paradiso* 27.[41] As Jeffrey Schnapp has noted, eclipses and crosses are linked implicitly in the central cantos of the *Paradiso*.[42] And in the *Vita nuova*, Dante uses the image of a darkened, sorrowing sun to reinforce the Christological significance of Beatrice's death.

> Poi me parve vedere a poco a poco
> turbar lo sole e apparir la stella,
> e pianger elli ed ella;
> cader li augelli volando per l'are,
> e la terra tremare;
> ed omo apparve scolorito e fioco,
> dicendomi: "Che fai? non sai novella?
> Morta è la donna tua, ch'era sì bella."
>
> (*V.N.* 23)

And then it seemed to me I saw the sun
grow slowly darker, and a star appear,
and sun and star did weep;
birds flying through the air fell dead to earth;
the earth began to quake.
A man appeared, pale, and his voice was weak
as he said to me: "You have not heard the news?
Your lady, once so lovely, now lies dead."

If this pattern of eclipses and crucifixions is, as I believe, deliberate, then it suggests another possible line of investigation. In addition to probing Dante's scientific method for its wit and humor, we should also be concerned, it seems, with the theological significance of the vanishing acts: the poet's erratic excursions into optics and astronomy are in some way connected to Christ's suffering on the Cross. To pursue this connection, let us turn our attention again to the Platonic creation myth.

In this myth, we recall, reason plays an unequivocally central role. Plato tells the story of the Demiurge to demonstrate that the physical universe is the work of a rational creator and that its movements are designed to teach men to think. The sun exists, he claims, so that man "might possess number" and might come to recognize the motion of the "same and uniform."

> The god kindled a light in the second orbit from the Earth—what we now call the Sun—in order that he might fill the whole heaven with his shining and that all living things from whom it was meet might possess number, learning it from the revolution of the Same and uniform. Thus and for these reasons day and night came into being, the period of the single and most intelligent revolution.[43]

The optimistic emphasis on order and rationality apparent in this myth is, no doubt, part of its appeal to Christian exegetes. Plato confirms their sense that God has placed his stamp on the heavens as a sign to man. Yet in absorbing this myth, the Christian exegete also complicates its original message. When the "*chi* in the sky" is converted into a cross, it takes on a set of darker associations that have no part in the *Timaeus*. The Christian cross may in some contexts serve as a sign of victory, peace, joy, and reconciliation, yet in a primary sense the Cross remains a sign of horrible suffering and unspeakable cruelty—a sign not only of the Resurrection but also of the Passion. It is, even more pertinently, a sign of reason's limitation—a sign that the Christian cosmos is more violent and more mysterious than that envisaged by any Greek philosopher. As Paul observes in Corinthians, clear-thinking Jews and Greeks cannot fail to stumble over the Cross; to them the idea of a god's death represents the height of "foolishness" (*stultitia*).

> Verbum enim crucis pereuntibus quidem stultitia est, his autem, qui salvi fiunt. . . . Iudeis quidem scandalum, gentibus autem stultitiam: ipsis autem vocatis, Iudaeis atque Graecis, Christum Dei virtutem et Dei sapientiam. (1 Cor. 1:18–24)

> For the doctrine of the cross is foolishness to those who perish, but to those who are saved, that is, to us, it is the power of God. . . . We preach a crucified Christ—to the Jews, indeed, a stumbling block and

to the Gentiles foolishness, but to those who are called both Jews and Greeks, Christ, the power of God and the wisdom of God.

The novel complexities of Christian cosmology—its emphasis on suffering and crisis—are apparent throughout the *Paradiso*, and especially in the cantos we have been considering. Beatrice, in canto 29, devotes less time to celebrating the angelic hierarchy than she does to commenting on various errors and disasters. First she corrects Jerome for having mistaken the date of the angels' creation. Next she discusses the fall of the rebel angels and Lucifer's "maladetto superbir." She then upbraids theologians for their "lying" theories of the Crucifixion eclipse and for their "piggish" greed. The rhetoric in cantos 2 and 10 is not nearly so violent and divisive, but the poet's interest in cosmic disorder is just as persistent. On entering the sphere of the sun, Dante draws our attention to the apparent misalignment of the celestial and planetary spheres, a misalignment that produces the "twisted path" of the zodiac and contributes to the erratic movements of the planets. In the sphere of the moon, Beatrice and Dante debate the causes of moonspots—the "dusty marks" that cause men on earth to doubt the perfection of the heavens and to tell the story of Cain ("di Cain favoleggiare," *Par.* 2.51). This discussion of the moon's apparent impurity in turn develops into a broader analysis of why the planets and the stars are not more uniform—why they are scattered so asymmetrically about the heavens and why their colors and intensities are so various (*Par.* 2.112–48).

There are, in fact, few cantos in the *Paradiso* where Dante does not address some type of error or disorder. The errors range from the cosmological variety—the precession of the equinoxes and the inequities of the Julian calendar—to historical examples—the sins of Boniface and the failure of Henry.[44] For a poem that is set in the heavens, the final cantica is surprisingly centered on failure and frustration. Yet if it is wrong to present Dante's cosmic vision as uniformly harmonious, it would also be wrong to label his cosmology discordant. As a general rule, the signs of disorder introduced into the *Paradiso* receive some form of positive resolution. This is certainly true of the errors and anomalies discussed in cantos 2, 10, and 29. The marks that mar the moon's surface are not interpreted by Beatrice as evidence of God's trembling hand, but as proof of heaven's vital diversity.[45]

The sun's erring motion, its wandering from the "straight path," is not construed as a failure on God's part to align the heavens properly, but as a productive, invigorating irregularity. The fall of the angels, man's expulsion from paradise, and Cain's slaying of Abel may, from a human perspective, seem to be unmixed disasters, but they are, the poet maintains, part of a "comic" plan. They are necessary episodes in a providential narrative where even original sin is said to function as a *felix culpa*. In the cosmology of the *Comedy*, threats to order are neither suppressed nor denied; instead, they are transformed and put to use. Violence, crisis, and disorder are reworked by the poet-cosmologist into the comic categories of play, diversity, and productive complexity.

I would like to think that the vanishing acts studied in this chapter represent the poetic equivalent of this basic cosmological principle. As Dante struggles to find a pattern that will redeem the disorder he finds in history and nature, so he designs a poem that allows his readers a similar imaginative engagement. The author of the *Paradiso* frustrates us in cantos 2, 10, and 29 so that we may eventually come to discover a beautifully articulated structure embracing nearly his entire invention. I voice this suggestion tentatively, not merely because it is a decidedly speculative account of Dante's methods, but also because it is a suspiciously benign account. If we do indeed decide to read the *Comedy* as Dante reads the cosmos, then we should expect to commit some of the same errors. We will not, perhaps, mislocate the moon or misread its spots, but we may well delude ourselves about the "perfect" order of the object we are studying.

Chapter 5

"O Brave Monster"

In the days when Vitruvius and Horace were the final arbiters of taste, and connoisseurs looked down their noses at "Gothic" art, it wasn't difficult to make sense of the medieval enthusiasm for monsters. Gargoyles, grotesques, green men, and griffins seemed ugly and ridiculous, but then so did much else medieval. The crowding of churches and poems with bizarre creatures was, for writers like Vasari, evidence of a general "licentiousness," their prominence one further proof of how much "confusion" and "artificiality" the medieval artist could tolerate.[1] Today, "Gothic" marvels present a much greater challenge. As scholars and art historians have rediscovered the harmony, coherence, and symmetry of medieval art and literature, the grotesque and gargoyle have come to seem genuinely monstrous. Shouldn't the "passion for order" that motivates art in the Middle Ages rule out the fantastic creatures that cavort at the edges of so many manuscripts? Can we explain away their outlandish shapes simply as "survivals" of primitive folk traditions, as Male suggests?[2] Are they merely marginal excesses? Or do they represent a significant counter-current within medieval aesthetics?

In this chapter I shall pose these questions about one marvel in particular: the human-headed, fur-covered serpent who carries Dante on his back deep into Hell. Geryon is, arguably, the

Comedy's most spectacular monster, and he is certainly one of the most disturbing. Though scholars have been unable to locate a source for Geryon's body, and though he thus seems to be one of the few creatures in Hell whose shape we can confidently attribute to Dante's imagination, he is not the kind of creature we would expect a theomimetic poet to invent.[3] His awkward, unnatural form seems to contradict the ordering, controlling impulse so evident elsewhere in Dante's art. The ride on Geryon is an episode that engages many of the central issues of earlier chapters, and it provides another chance to consider the roles of disorder, error, play, and daring within the *Comedy*.

The first thing one notices about Geryon is the elaborate staging of his entrance. Blocked in their descent through Hell by a steep cliff, the travelers halt at its edge and peer into an abyss. Virgil asks Dante to loosen a cord from his waist (a cord we didn't know he was wearing), which Virgil throws over the side without any explanation. Then, apparently in response to this strange signal, Geryon slowly rises out of the depths. Dante does not rush to display the monster's body; instead, he pauses to discuss his position as narrator. Geryon is so peculiar a creature that he makes the poet nervous. Dante is afraid, he claims, that his readers won't believe what he has to say, and he swears, by the "notes" of his own poem, that he is telling the truth:

> Sempre a quel ver c'ha faccia di menzogna
> de' l'uom chiuder le labbra fin ch'el puote,
> però che sanza colpa fa vergogna;
> ma qui tacer nol posso; e per le note
> di questa comedìa, lettor, ti giuro,
> s'elle non sien di lunga grazia vòte,
> ch'i' vidi per quell'aere grosso e scuro
> venir notando una figura in suso,
> maravigliosa ad ogne cor sicuro.
>
> (*Inf.* 16.124–32)

To that truth which has the face of a lie a man should always close his lips so far as he can, for through no fault of his it brings reproach; but here I cannot be silent; and, reader, I swear to you by the notes of this Comedy—so may they not fail of lasting favor—that I saw, through that thick and murky air, come swimming upwards a figure amazing to every steadfast heart.

I will have occasion later to comment on the curious phrasing of this promise, but for now I merely want to draw attention to its function as a delaying tactic, a device for keeping the monster offstage and generating suspense. In many types of narrative, such an artful use of an aside would be unremarkable; we expect from many authors leisured indirection, particularly if it comes at moments of erotic stimulation or physical peril. But we do not expect this kind of delay from Dante, and so his handling of Geryon comes as something of a surprise. With the monster's entrance into the poem, the poet seems to have wandered into a different genre; he seems to have strayed, for a moment, from his dense, economical methods of narration into a more sinuous style, a style with strong affiliations to romance.[4]

We see the same type of generic digression in the representation of the monster's body. While Dante generally limits descriptive passages to a few choice phrases or a single telling detail, he presents Geryon's features with studied thoroughness. He begins by showing us the monster's face, then moves on to his serpentine torso, his paws, his hairy arms, and his magnificently colored back, chest, and sides:

> E quella sozza imagine di froda
> sen venne, e arrivò la testa e 'l busto,
> ma 'n su la riva non trasse la coda.
> La faccia sua era faccia d'uom giusto,
> tanto benigna avea di fuor la pelle,
> e d'un serpente tutto l'altro fusto;
> due branche avea pilose insin l'ascelle;
> lo dosso e'l petto e ambedue le coste
> dipinti avea di nodi e di rotelle.

> Con più color, sommesse e sovraposte
> non fer mai drappi Tartari né Turchi,
> né fuor tai telle per Aragne imposte.
>   (*Inf.* 17.7–18)

And that foul image of fraud came onward and landed his head and chest, but he did not draw his tail onto the bank. His face was the face of a just man, so benign was its outward aspect, and all his trunk was serpentine; he had two paws, hairy to the armpits; his back and breast and both his sides were painted with knots and circles. Tartars or Turks never made cloth with more colors of groundwork and pattern, nor were such webs laid on the loom by Arachne.

One could argue that this unusual dilation is necessary in order to convey Geryon's monstrosity—it is the very systematic nature of the description that reveals the lack of system in the body being represented—if it were not for the final terzina, in which Dante pauses to admire the coat's pattern and its color. The comparisons to Turkish carpets and to the weaving of Arachne locate the passage within the space of the marvelous. Dante is not merely showing us the beast, he is slowing his narrative to give us time to wonder.

Even the most active section of the poet's encounter with Geryon—the flight on the monster's back—is marked by such indirections and diversions. To build up suspense, Dante defers his approach to the fierce beast in favor of a second encounter: while Virgil stops to converse (silently) with Geryon, Dante walks ahead to discuss usury with a collection of well-roasted bankers. This is the only time in the *Inferno* that Dante confronts sinners alone and one of the very few occasions when he must retrace his footsteps in order to move forward. The shape of the digression is unique, and in a poem where motion is so insistently allegorical, where progression means progress and inversion signifies conversion, even such an apparently innocuous loop catches our attention and invites speculation.[5] After Dante returns from his conversation with the usurers, we approach the climax toward which the canto has slowly been building: the moment when Dante will climb onto the monster and descend into the Malebolge. Now it is the traveler's fear—and the poet's description of that fear—that delays and distracts. First Dante compares himself to a fever victim, shivering and pale; next his voice dies away in terror; then he asks us to remember Icarus and Phaeton and declares their fear of flying to be no greater than his; finally, near the end of the flight, he dares to peer down into the depths, only to become even more frightened at seeing the fires and hearing the cries of the damned. Nowhere in the *Comedy* (except perhaps in the representation of Satan) is so much space devoted to describing terror. The process of mounting the beast and descending into Hell takes very nearly half a canto and, in my eyes at least, is unrivaled in terms of suspense, adventure, and high fantasy. This is as close as we come in the *Comedy* to a ride on a flying carpet.

Though every reader will naturally have his or her own response, I think it is safe to say that the meeting with the monster is one of the most memorable episodes in the *Comedy*, in part because it is essentially incongruous—a wavering, looping strand set into a text in which the narrative threads are all drawn taut.[6] But it is not only the episode's unusual composition that gives it prominence. Our attention is also focused on the encounter by the *Inferno*'s formal architecture. The same flight that carries the travelers across the most pronounced physical barrier in the infernal landscape—the steep cliff leading down to the Malebolge—carries us across the mathematical midpoint of the first cantica—the gap between the seventeenth and eighteenth cantos.[7]

This central niche would exist whether or not Dante had invented Geryon, but it is clear that the monster is placed there deliberately. There can be little doubt on this point, because the monster's central position is reinforced by one of those subtle symmetries that critics take such pride and pleasure in discovering. In this case, the symmetrical pattern involves three symbols of fraud—three silent fur-covered beasts that block, twist, and invert the path of the poet's progress. One of these silent symbols leaps out in the first canto—the lonza; one stands fixed in the last canto—Satan; and one swims lazily toward the poet at the *Inferno*'s center. At each encounter the same introductory formula (*ecco . . . ecco . . .*) is repeated:

> Ed *ecco*, quasi al cominciar de l'erta,
>   una lonza leggiera e presta molto,
>   che di pel macolato era coverta.
>
>   (*Inf.* 1.31–33)

> *Ecco* la fiera con la coda aguzza,
>   che passa i monti e rompe i muri e l'armi!
> *Ecco* colei che tutto 'l mondo appuzza!
>
>   (*Inf.* 17.1–3)

> D'innanzi mi si tolse e fé restarmi,
>   "*Ecco* Dite," dicendo, "ed *ecco* il loco
>   ove convien di fortezza t'armi."
>
>   (*Inf.* 34.19–21)

And *behold*, near the beginning of the steep, a leopard light-footed and very fleet, covered with a spotted hide!

Behold the beast with the pointed tail, that passes mountains and breaks walls and weapons! *Behold* him that infects all the world!

He stepped aside and made me stop, saying, "*Behold* Dis!—and *behold* the place where you must arm yourself with fortitude."

These broad similarities among the silent symbols of fraud branch into more specific iconographic correspondences: the same rope belt employed in an unsuccessful attempt to catch the lonza is hurled into the depths of the Malebolge to summon Geryon; the same adjective that describes the lonza's spotted fur (*dipinto*) also describes Geryon's woven coat; the same image (and rhyme) that Dante uses to describe Satan—his "ladder" out of Hell—is used to describe Geryon's role as a "ladder" into the Malebolge:

> Omai si scende per sì fatte *scale*;
>   monta dinanzi, ch'i' voglio esser mezzo,
>   sì che la coda non possa far *male*.
>
>   (*Inf.* 17.82–84)

"Attienti ben, ché per cotali *scale*,"
  disse 'l maestro, ansando com'uom lasso,
"conviensi dipartir da tanto *male*."
  (*Inf.* 34.82–84)

Now the descent is by such stairs as these. Mount in front, for I wish to be between, so that the tail may not harm you.

"Cling fast," said the master, panting like a weary man, "for by such stairs as these we must depart from so much evil."

Comparing the three beasts, we realize that Dante has used them to articulate the outline of his poem. He has framed the journey through Hell with a pair of beasts and placed the third beast at the journey's middle. The flight on the monster's back becomes the central term in a rigorously symmetric pattern.

Flight
Lonza — 17 cantos —   on   — 17 cantos — Satan
Geryon

Pressing into a more speculative region, we can even see this symmetry worked out in the *Comedy*'s rhyme scheme. When Dante describes the lonza's bright, painted fur and Satan's shaggy flanks, the terms *pelle* and *coste* serve as rhyme-words; the same words and rhymes are interwoven in the description of Geryon and his tapestrylike fur.

Sì ch'a bene sperar m'era cagione
  di quella fiera a la gaetta *pelle*
l'ora del tempo e la dolce stagione.
  (*Inf.* 1.41–43)

La faccia sua era faccia d'uom giusto,
  tanto benigna avea di fuor la *pelle*,
e d'un serpente tutto l'altro fusto;
due branche avea pilose insin l'*ascelle*;
  lo dosso e'l petto e ambedue le *coste*
dipinti avea di nodi e di *rotelle*.
Con più color, sommesse e *sovraposte*
  non fer mai drappi Tartai né Turchi,
né fuor tai telle per Aragne *imposte*.
  (*Inf.* 17.10–18)

> ed el prese di tempo e loco *poste*,
> e quando l'ali fuoro aperte assai,
> appigliò sé a le vellute *coste*.
>
> (*Inf.* 34.71–73)

This kind of subtle symmetry would appear to be more typical of Dante's art than the suspense-generating delays discussed earlier. The existence of a veiled pattern confirms our sense of the poet's general enthusiasm for formal structures and reminds us of his immense control over his artifice, a control few critics can resist celebrating. Grandgent speaks for the majority of Dante scholars when he lavishly praises the *Comedy* for its "wonderful" order:

Of the external attributes of the *Divine Comedy*, the most wonderful is its symmetry. With all its huge bulk and bewildering multifarious detail, it is as sharply planned as a Gothic cathedral. Dante had the very uncommon power of fixing his attention upon the part without losing sight of the whole: every incident, every character receives its peculiar development, but at the same time is made to contribute its exact share to the total effect. The more one studies the poem, the clearer become its general lines, the more intricate its correspondences, the more elaborate its climaxes.[8]

Yet our discovery of this particular structure does have its surprises. One might question, for example, Dante's decision to put Geryon—a fantastic creature of romance—at the center of so elaborate a symmetry. Geryon is, after all, a monster; he is made of parts that do not quite fit together, yet he is being used to knit together Dante's poem. As Dante depends on Geryon to carry him into the Malebolge, so he also seems to depend on the monster to support his poem's symmetric structure. Adjusting Grandgent's architectural metaphor to suit this particular occasion, we might compare the *Inferno* to a Gothic cathedral where the central panel in the central portal reveals not Christ in His glory but the weirdest of gargoyles.

At the start of this chapter, I noted that the prominence of gargoyles and grotesques in medieval art and literature has been something of an embarrassment to modern art historians and literary critics. In fact, monsters were a problem much earlier. Already in the twelfth century, Bernard was bothered enough by the architectural grotesques in Cluniac churches to plead for their removal:

But in the cloister, under the eyes of the Brethren who read there, what profit is there in those ridiculous monsters, in that marvelous and deformed comeliness, that comely deformity ("deformis formositas, ac formosa deformitas")? To what purpose are those unclean apes, those fierce lions, those monstrous centaurs, those half-men, those striped tigers, those fighting knights, those hunters winding their horns? Many bodies are there seen under one head, or again, many heads to a single body. Here is a four-footed beast with a serpent's tail; there, a fish with a beast's head. Here again the forepart of a horse trails after a goat behind it, or a horned beast bears the hinder parts of a horse. In short so many and so marvelous are the varieties of divers shapes on every hand, that we are more tempted to read in the marble than in our books, and to spend the whole day in wondering at these things rather than in meditating on the law of God. For God's sake, if men are not ashamed of these follies, why at least do they not shrink from the expense?[9]

Augustine, too, was troubled by monstrosities, though of a slightly different type. Whereas Bernard worried over the fantastic inventions of human artists, Augustine worried over God's: the Hermaphrodites, who "exercise in turn the male and female functions in begetting and bearing offspring"; the Pygmies, who are "no more than a few feet high"; the Sciopodes, who have but one leg and use their broad umbrellalike feet to block the summer sun; the Cynocephalae, "whose doglike heads and barking voices prove they are more like animals than men"; and a host of unnamed wonders—men whose feet grow backwards, men who have single eyes in the middle of their foreheads, men who breathe only through their ears. Augustine warns readers of the *City of God* not to misinterpret such ugly creatures. It would be a crime, he insists, to imagine, even for a moment, that their distorted shapes are evidence of God's incompetence. If they seem to us to be monstrous failures, it is because we have not visualized the total pattern of creation. Even the neckless marvels whose eyes peer from their shoulders have a place in God's plan:

God is the creator of all; He knows best where and when and what is, or was, best for Him to create, since He deliberately fashioned the beauty of the whole out of both the similarity and dissimilarity of its parts. The trouble with a person who does not see the whole is that he is offended by the ugliness of a part because he does not know its context of relation to the whole.[10]

Bernard's effort to banish monsters and Augustine's effort to redeem them suggest two possible explanations for Geryon's centrality. Following Augustine, one could argue that it is the total pattern of the poem that matters and that Geryon's ugliness is only a local disturbance. When we step back, we see that even this apparently incoherent creature is part of the "beauty of the whole." Following Bernard, we might place the emphasis rather differently. Instead of claiming that ugliness is redeemed, we might ask whether the ugly monster's central position isn't a sign of the poet's anxiety. When Bernard decries the presence of grotesques in Cluniac carvings, he is complaining not merely about their ugliness but about their "deformis formositas, ac formosa deformitas." He is worried less about the monsters' repulsiveness than about their power to attract and distract monks from their books. The monster, one might hypothesize, is a figure not for a technical aesthetic failure—a clumsy sculpture, an awkward rhyme—but for a failure of art to serve a sanctioned purpose: art gone astray.[11] For reasons that will take some time to elaborate, I believe that Bernard's more ambivalent attitude toward monsters is a better guide to Dante's.

Let me begin by returning to the poet's odd promise to tell

the truth about Geryon: "Per le note / di questa comedìa, let-tor, ti giuro." This oath is odd, less for its falsehood, which we could excuse as conventional, than for its circularity and its in-sistence: Dante swears by his poem that what his poem tells us is true; he speaks within fiction in defense of the fiction of truth-telling; a work of *alto ingegno*—a *comedìa*—is sworn upon as if it were a bible. Such a manifestly unconvincing (yet passion-ately voiced) plea puts us, as readers, in an ambiguous posi-tion. Though we certainly haven't believed what the poet has told us of his journey up to this point, we might have assumed that we were supposed to suspend our disbelief.[12] Now it ap-pears that we can't be so sure. Dante seems, at this moment, to be playing at truth-telling in a deliberately suspicious manner. He seems to encourage us to smile conspiratorially at his splendid deceitfulness, or, at the very least, to bring our doubts about his fiction back into focus. Such doubts become irre-pressible when we learn that the incredible monster the poet has sworn to be honest about is, in fact, a personification of Fraud—"[la] sozza imagine di froda." Fraud is a category of sin that embraces crimes as disparate as adultery, treachery, bar-ratry, and simony, but it is also the category in which fiction might conceivably be placed. Imaginative literature, as stern moralists are prone to observe, is a form of deception. In the *Convivio*, Dante himself goes so far as to refer to certain select varieties of poetry—the myths of Ovid and other secular fab-ulists—as "beautiful lies."[13] Far from pushing this disquieting association from our minds, Dante's promise to tell the truth about Fraud pushes it under our noses. In swearing by the notes of his *Comedy*, Dante creates two symmetric spheres of action. In one sphere, a traveler confronts a monster representing Fraud; in the other, a poet confronts an audience that accuses him, at least in his imagination, of fraud.

This symmetry is so strongly suggested at the start of the ep-isode that several readers have been tempted to look for signs of it elsewhere. Ascoli, for example, has drawn attention to the spiral trajectory followed by Geryon during his descent.[14] At

one point Dante compares the monster's wheeling motion to
that of a falcon circling above its master:

> E vidi poi, ché nol vedea davanti,
>   lo scendere e 'l girar per li gran mali
>   che s'appressavan da diversi canti.
> Come 'l falcon ch'è stato assai su l'ali,
>   che sanza veder logoro o uccello
>   fa dire al falconiere "Omè, tu cali!"
> discende lasso onde si move isnello,
>   per cento rote, e da lunge si pone
>   dal suo maestro, disdegnoso e fello . . .
>
> (*Inf.* 17.124–32)

And I saw then—for I had not seen it before—the descending and
the circling through the great evils that were drawing near on every
side. As the falcon that has been long on the wing—that, without seeing
lure or bird, makes the falconer cry, "Ah, ah, you're coming down!"—
descends weary, with many a wheeling, to where it set out swiftly, and
alights disdainful and sullen, far from its master . . .

This simile reminds us of Geryon's wonderful strangeness: he
is a creature who flies without wings and who moves at once
like a bird and like a swimmer. But the simile also recalls an-
other spiral trajectory: the course of the poet's journey toward
God. After being pushed back from the sunlit mountain in *In-
ferno* 1, Dante is forced to move ahead by moving in circles: he
spirals into Hell, he winds his way up Mount Purgatory, and he
arcs his way across the wide open spaces of Paradise. Geryon's
"cento rote" through the "diversi canti" of Hell could be viewed
as merely a subsection of this larger spiral, or they could be
viewed as a restaging of the journey in miniature—a narrative
mise-en-abîme in which the traveler's flight on Fraud stands for
the poet's daring flight of imagination. The indirection of the
monster's passage would, in such a reading, mark the indirec-
tion of fiction itself. Neither frauds nor storytellers, so the ar-
gument runs, travel in perfectly straight lines.

Another suggestive moment is the systematic description of
the monster's physical appearance at the start of canto 17.

Geryon is, for didactic reasons, supposed to be ugly; as the "sozza imagine di froda" he represents the gravest sin punished in Hell. Yet there are hints that the poet is rather proud of Geryon and his confusing assortment of limbs. The adjective *aguzza*, which is used to describe Geryon's pointed tail, can mean "astute" as well as "sharp," and comes, in literary circles, to mean "wit."[15] The fur coat that covers his chest and flanks is compared not to an animal's rough hide but to a brightly colored tapestry. *Color* is the standard praise-word for rhetorical ornament, and woven tapestries are standard symbols for written texts. Weaving can stand, as it does in the *Odyssey*, for narrative deferment or development; it can stand, as it does in the *Convivio*, for allegory; or it can stand, as it does in the *De vulgari*, for the art of linking lines of verse together:

Videtur nobis hec quam habitudinem dicimus maxima pars eius quod artis est. Hec etenim circa cantus divisionem atque *contextum* carminum et rithimorum relationem consistit. (*De vulgari* 2.11.1)

It seems to me that what I call arrangement constitutes the greatest part of what pertains to art, because the division of the melody as well as the *weaving* together of the lines and the setting in relation of the rhymes are based on it.

The monster's body may be a clumsy pastiche, but his textile-like fur suggests an artistic performance of immense coherence and control. The pattern on Geryon's back is, we are told, unequaled even by Arachne's tapestries, and those were, even by Minerva's high standards, faultless.

The self-reflexivity of Dante's ride on Fraud is further underscored by the episode's distinctive citational context. Apart from the cantos of the thieves, the encounter with Geryon is the section of the *Comedy* richest in allusions to Ovid. In the space of one canto Dante alludes to the *Metamorphoses* three times. First he compares Geryon's coat to Arachne's flawless tapestries. Then he compares his fear of flying on Geryon with the fear experienced by Phaeton and Icarus, the two daredevils who fall to their deaths in books 2 and 8 of the *Metamorphoses*:

> Maggior paura non credo che fosse
>   quando Fetonte abbandonò li freni,
>   per che 'l ciel, come pare ancor, si cosse;
> né quando Icaro misero le reni
>   sentì spennar per la scaldata cera,
>   gridando il padre a lui "Mala via tieni!"
> che fu la mia, quando vidi ch'i' era
>   ne l'aere d'ogne parte, e vidi spenta
>   ogne veduta fuor che de la fera.
>
> (*Inf.* 17.106–14)

I do not think that there was greater fear when Phaeton let loose the reins, for which the sky still appears scorched, nor when the wretched Icarus felt his loins unfeathering by the melting wax, and his father cried to him, "You go an ill way!" than was mine when I saw extinguished every sight save the beast.

The *Metamorphoses* is a critical text to find cited here because it is virtually a textbook on the art of specular narration. Among the hundreds of narratives imbedded in Ovid's sprawling poem, dozens reflect his experience as poet. In some cases this is because the stories are about ingenious artists like Orpheus and Daedalus; in others it is because the stories are about extraordinary acts of human daring like the flights of Phaeton and Icarus. This aspect of the *Metamorphoses* was not lost on later writers. In the hands of Chaucer and Guillaume de Lorris, the Ovidian hero becomes a vehicle for establishing a poetic identity: Chaucer identifies himself with Apollo's gossiping crow and Guillaume with Narcissus.[16] Dante may claim Virgil as his teacher, but like Chaucer and Guillaume he relies primarily on Ovid at moments of poetic self-definition.[17]

The invocations to the *Purgatorio* and the *Paradiso* are two such moments. At the start of each cantica, Dante calls on a god to help him and, in the process, names a rebellious Ovidian artist whom that god had punished. In the *Purgatorio*, the poet recalls the nine daughters of Pierus, who challenged the Muses in song and were transformed, after their defeat, into magpies.[18]

Ma qui la morta poesì resurga,
  o sante Muse, poi che vostro sono;
  e qui Caliopè alquanto surga,
seguitando il mio canto con quel suono
  di cui le Piche misere sentiro
  lo colpo tal, che disperar perdono.
(Purg. 1.7–12)

But here let dead poetry rise again, O holy Muses, since I am yours; and here let Calliope also rise up, following my song with that music whose force so struck the wretched Pies that they despaired of pardon.

In the *Paradiso*, he names the pipe-playing Marsyas, the rival of Apollo who was flayed by the god for his musical ambitions.

O buono Appollo, a l'ultimo lavoro
  fammi del tuo valor sì fatto vaso,
  come dimandi a dar l'amato alloro.
Infino a qui l'un giogo di Parnaso
  assai mi fu; ma or con amendue
  m'è uopo intrar ne l'aringo rimaso.
Entra nel petto mio, e spira tue
  sì come quando Marsia traesti
  de la vagina de le membra sue.
(Par. 1.13–21)

O good Apollo, for this last labor make me such a vessel of your worth as you require for granting your beloved laurel. Thus far the one peak of Parnassus has sufficed me, but now I have need of both, as I enter the arena that remains. Enter into my breast and breathe there as when you drew Marsyas from the sheath of his limbs.

If the rhetorical structure of these invocations suggests humility—a call for help from the gods—the poet's decision to return to the *Metamorphoses* suggests something quite different. The stories of Marsyas and the Pierides, like the stories of Icarus, Phaeton, and Arachne, are about competition, struggle, and daring rebellion. Their art does not represent a humble imitation of divine creativity, but a potentially dangerous contest with divinity. Moreover, the phrasing of the invocations tends to identify Dante with the rebellious human artist: Calliope is to "follow" ("seguitando") his song much as she followed the songs of the Pierides in their unequal competition; Apollo is to inspire the poet—to enter his chest and breathe there—just as he breathed when stripping Marsyas of his skin. In setting out to write the *Comedy*'s two final cantiche, Dante uses Ovid to assert the extraordinary boldness of his project and the risks it entails.[19]

The outlandish promise of truth-telling, the spiral trajectory, the woven fabric, and the multiple Ovidian allusions all suggest that we read the encounter with Geryon as a meditation on poetry. And this brings Dante in line with Bernard. The poet, like the theologian, finds in the fascinating but fear-provoking shape of a monster a vehicle for outlining art's hazards. He uses Geryon to show us fiction's proximity to fraud, its perilous attractiveness, and its susceptibility to perversion. It is possible that other medieval monsters serve similar purposes. One might speculate, for example, that the architectural grotesque functions as the cathedral's parodic double—a figure for the constructive, synthetic impulse gone awry. But whether or not medieval monsters have such a universal meaning, it is clear that they are used by Dante and Bernard to represent widely shared concerns. Although we may wholeheartedly celebrate the accomplishments of medieval writers and artists, although we may enjoy their works with unmixed pleasure, their own relation to their creative achievements was far more ambivalent. Augustine, we recall, repents his early training in rhetoric and the tears he shed as a youth over Dido. Boethius, sick in prison, listens enraptured to the Muses, only to banish them as strumpets. Chaucer writes the *Canterbury Tales* with what seems to be evident delight and then retracts the most engaging: the tales that "sounen into sinne."

Dante clearly belongs in this tradition, and it is not only the flight on Geryon that places him there. One need only consider the fates of Francesca, Oderisi, and Brunetto Latini to realize that, within the fictive world of the *Comedy*, art is a dangerous undertaking, both for those who produce works and for those who enjoy them. Yet I feel we also need to be cautious in our gauging of Dante's anxieties. It is worth remembering that just as there is a difference between fiction and reality, so there is also a difference between the doctrine expressed in a poem and a poet's sentiments. Dante may repeatedly portray the perils of aesthetic pleasure, but it does not necessarily follow that he is actually afraid for himself or for his readers. In dramatizing the dangers of literary error, he could be simply seeking to write a more compelling, more exciting poem—a poem in which the gap between reading and misreading stretches between Heaven and Hell, and in which the reader and the poet are always (at least fictionally) at risk. In such an account, Dante merely exploits the medieval ambivalence about the place of the artist; he manipulates, manages, and stages anxieties rather than actually experiencing them.[20]

To cast such doubts on Dante's sincerity might seem impertinent were it not that his model for transgressive poetry is Ovid. In the work of the Latin poet, there is also a great show of anxiety about the proper limits of human art; in the *Metamorphoses* the gods repeatedly punish mortals for their arrogant delight in their artistic achievements. Yet it would be a mistake to conclude that such tales of punished transgression are evidence of piety or humility. Most readers of the *Metamorphoses* would, I think, agree that the fiction of divine punishment is manipulated by Ovid purely for pleasure.

One of these pleasures is the sport of dressing up in heroes' clothing, of disguising (and then revealing) the poet's craft in scenes of sculpting, weaving, and flight. When Arachne and Minerva compete, Ovid cleverly turns their looms into lyres. The shrill threads and busy fingers of the weavers seem, for a moment, to belong to a pair of musicians singing about metamorphosis:[21]

> Haud mora, constituunt diversis partibus ambae
> et gracili geminas intendunt stamine telas:
> tela iugo vincta est, stamen secernit harundo,

inseritur medium radiis subtemen acutis,
quod digiti expediunt, atque inter stamina ductum
percusso feriunt insecti pectine dentes.

(Met. 6.53–58)

They both take their separate places without delay and they stretch
the fine warp each upon her loom. The web is bound upon the beam,
the reed separates the threads of the warp, the woof is threaded
through by the sharp shuttles which their busy fingers ply, the notched
teeth of the hammering slay beat the woof into place as it is shot be-
tween the threads of the web.

When describing the waxen wings that will carry Icarus to his
death, Ovid again playfully interjects himself. The wings shaped
by the master artificer are eventually compared to a pair of bird's
wings, but first they are likened to a musical instrument—a set
of "rustic" pan-pipes:

Dixit et ignotas animum dimittit in artes
naturamque novat. nam ponit in ordine pennas,
a minima coeptas, longam breviore sequenti
ut clivo crevisse putes: sic rustica quondam
fistula disparibus paulatim surgit avenis.

(Met. 8.188–92)

So saying, he sets his mind at work upon unknown arts, and changes
the laws of nature. For he lays feathers in order, beginning at the
smallest, short next to long, so that you would think they had grown
upon a slope. Just so the old-fashioned rustic pan-pipes with their
unequal reeds rise one above another.

When Phaeton first glimpses the temple of his father Phoebus,
Ovid characterizes its artistry using a formula that has often been
taken as a statement of his own goals as a poet: "materiam su-
perabat opus"—"his art conquered the subject matter" (Met.
2.5).[22]

A second kind of pleasure derives from the complex tonali-
ties that such stories make possible. On one level, the stories
are full of terror, foreboding, and self-doubt. When Marsyas is
skinned, when Phaeton is roasted in the sun, and when Icarus
tumbles headlong toward the sea, Ovid plays up the horror of

their suffering. He counts (or at least imagines counting) Marsyas's trembling entrails; he pauses to describe the smell of Phaeton's burning skin. Yet even as Ovid exacts the cruelest punishments on his daredevil doubles, he makes it clear that he is not terrified himself, that he enjoys counting the entrails, and that the failed artists are to be respected even in their failure. Arachne's metamorphic tapestry is so wonderfully executed that even Minerva and Envy cannot fault it: "Non illud Pallas, non illud carpere Livor / possit opus" (*Met.* 6.129–30). On Phaeton's tomb, the Naiads carve an epitaph that both laments and celebrates his journey: "Hic situs est Phaethon currus auriga paterni / quem si non tenuit magnis tamen excidit ausis" (*Met.* 2.327–28). When Icarus and Daedalus fly out over the Aegean, a series of more humble artisans clutching plows, crooks, and fishing poles (poor substitutes for pointed pens) mistake the winged pair for gods:[23]

> Hos aliquis, tremula dum captat harundine pisces,
> aut pastor baculo stivave innixus arator
> vidit et obstipuit, quique aethera carpere possent,
> credidit esse deos.
>
> (*Met.* 8.217–20)

Now some fisherman spies them, angling for fish with his flexible rod, or a shepherd, leaning upon his crook, or a plowman, on his plowhandles—spies them and stands stupefied, and believes them to be gods that they can fly through the air.

The stories of Arachne, Icarus, and Phaeton officially teach us about the dangers of overaspiration; implicitly they celebrate the failed overachiever.

The same delight in danger can be discerned in many of the *Comedy*'s Ovidian moments, and it is especially evident in the encounter with Geryon. When the monster first enters the poem, Dante insists that he is a nervous, reluctant narrator. He swears that he has not created the strange beast and that he writes about him under compulsion. This show of reluctance in no way dampens our pleasure in the episode—or, I suspect, the poet's pleasure. Even as Dante professes to be terrified by

Geryon, he makes it clear that this monster represents an imaginative tour de force: Geryon is, he announces, something altogether new—"novità"—and his strange shape is, he declares, "maravigliosa." The longer Dante delays, the more fear he professes, the more anxious we are to see the monster, and the more ready we are to enjoy his horribleness. Closer contact between beast and poet only sharpens the contradictions in Dante's pose. When he mounts on Geryon's back, Dante professes to be so terrified that he shakes like a fever victim; he tells us that he is so scared that he cannot even call out to Virgil for help.

> Qual è colui che sì presso ha 'l riprezzo
> de la quartana, c'ha già l'unghie smorte,
> e triema tutto pur guardando 'l rezzo,
> tal divenn' io a le parole porte;
> ma vergogna mi fé le sue minacce,
> che innanzi a buon segnor fa servo forte.
> I' m'assettai in su quelle spallacce;
> sì volli dir, ma la voce non venne
> com'io credetti: "Fa che tu m'abbracce."
> *(Inf.* 17.85–93)

As one who has the shivering-fit of the quartan so near that his nails are already pale, and he trembles all over at the mere sight of shade, such I became at these words of his; but shame rebuked me, which makes a servant brave in the presence of a good master. I seated myself on those ugly shoulders, and I wanted to say (but the voice did not come as I thought), "See that you embrace me!"

For all the fear and trembling attributed to the *traveler*, the *poet* hardly seems tongue-tied or terrified. Indeed, there are few passages in the *Comedy* where Dante allows himself to exaggerate and elaborate so freely. The image of the silent poet descending on the back of the monster reflects imaginative exuberance rather than modesty. In staging the anxiety of transgression, Dante, like Ovid, shows no signs of actually suffering from it.

Dante could conceivably be unaware of how closely his posture resembles Ovid's; he could be hoping, as many critics have suggested, that his readers will identify him as a different, humbler kind of poet.[24] But I think it more likely that Dante recognizes his affinity with the Latin poet and that he enters into a playful and admiring rivalry with him. It is worth noting that all the Ovidian allusions in cantos 16 and 17 measure Dante's inventions and experience against his Latin predecessor's: the "color" of Geryon's fur is no less bright than Arachne's tapestry; Dante's "fear" (and, by extension, his daring) is no less than Icarus's or Phaeton's. Even Dante's polemical silencing of Ovid in the circle of the thieves seems to reflect an admiring acceptance of the earlier poet's genius. It is surely an homage to Ovid's wit and skill at wordplay that Dante chooses to rhyme "Ovidio" with "invidio":

> Taccia di Cadmo e d'Aretusa *Ovidio*,
>   ché se qello in serpente e quella in fonte
>   converte poetando, io non lo '*nvidio*;
> ché due nature mai a fronte a fronte
>   non trasmutò sì ch'amendue le forme
>   a cambiar lor matera fosser pronte.
>   (*Inf.* 25.97–102)

Concerning Cadmus and Arethusa let Ovid be silent, for if he, poetizing, converts the one into a serpent and the other into a fountain, I do not envy him; for two natures front to front he never so transmuted that both forms were prompt to exchange their substance.

Reading in the Asylum

The official subject of this study has been Dante's errors, but I have not hesitated to point out other kinds of error as well. In the guise of a white-coated ophthalmologist I have probed the *Comedy*'s exegetical tradition in search of cataracts and myopia. I would like to think that my aim in doing so has been analytic rather than strictly corrective—I have tried to show that our blunders are, on occasion, as revelatory as Dante's—yet I am sure there are points where my interest (even enthusiasm) for readerly error has led me astray. At the very least, my effort to describe general trends and broad interpretive strategies has tended to wash out nuance and subtlety; the chief virtue of most critical studies consists in details, which for the sake of clarity I have often been compelled to neglect. Although I can't now make amends for all such oversights, I would like to use these last paragraphs to offer a brief, belated apology to one particular group of slighted critics: those to whom time and fashion have already been more than sufficiently unkind.

I regret, for instance, that my analysis of the *Vita nuova*'s hidden symmetry relied so heavily on Singleton's writings and that I mentioned only in passing the scholar who actually discovered it: Gabriele Rossetti. To the extent that Rossetti's name is familiar today, it is largely due to the reputations of his brilliant children—Dante and Christina—and his own reputation for interpretive extravagance. When Rossetti's work is cited in historical surveys, he is portrayed as an imaginative critic who at some point in his career slipped from ingenious idiosyncrasy into mere delusion. Rossetti's most ambitious project—his five-volume *Il mistero dell' amor platonico*—is probably the work that lies farthest from the border.[1] A far-ranging study of the ancient origins of Masonic societies, *Il mistero* expresses Rossetti's belief that the *Vita nuova* and the *Comedy* are really secret political manifestos addressed to an elect masonic circle that, according to conventional histories of Freemasonry, did not yet exist. This project so distressed those closest to Rossetti that they did their best to suppress it: his friends conspired together to prevent its distribution in England, and immediately after his death, his devoted wife Francesca gathered together surviving copies of *Il mistero* and had them burnt.[2] It is in *Il mistero* that Rossetti first publicly announces the "secret pattern" of the *Vita nuova*, the pattern Singleton later used to launch his famous career.

I also wish I had discussed more fully and more generously Giovanni Agnelli, the amateur *dantista* who produced his splendid maps of Hell while working at an institute for deaf-mutes. From my brief allusions to Agnelli in Chapter Two, it might have seemed that I was having fun at Agnelli's expense, exploiting his marginal position to discredit his claims. In fact, what initially attracted me to Agnelli was his exemplarity rather than his oddity. The *Comedy* has always been popular with outsiders and exiles, hardened convicts and political prisoners, marooned Victorians and American academics. It is chance, but perhaps not only chance, that in the very years during which Agnelli penned his *Topo-cronografia*, another teacher in an institute for deaf-mutes on the other side of the Atlantic produced a verbal map of the *Comedy*—the poem's first concordance.[3]

When originally planning this study, I had intended to give Rossetti and Agnelli far greater prominence. But in the course of plotting my arguments, I discovered that finding a place for these eccentric readers was much more difficult than I had anticipated. I discovered that I could not devote space to their "bizarre" and "pathetic" projects without casting suspicion on my own efforts and those of my more illustrious predecessors. Their evidently obsessive search for secret patterns, hidden structures, and perfect symmetries threatened to reveal how strange a poet Dante is and how peculiar our responses to his poetry have been. In order to present myself and my colleagues as sober, sensible researchers into literary history, it proved far safer to quote from distinguished authorities such as Landino, Singleton, Moore, and Padoan than to engage critics clearly working at the edge.

This was a disappointing discovery for me to make because I have argued throughout these chapters that we should enjoy the fluid boundary between error and insight, celebrate interpretive extravagance, and avoid a narrowing insistence on orthodoxy. Having failed to find space for oddballs like Rossetti and Agnelli, I realize now that it is much easier to voice such principles than to follow them, easier to imagine a disinterested reading than to perform one. Though one may begin a long analytic project convinced that all interpretive paths deserve attention, time wears down one's resistance. Positions adopted for the sake of argument or elegance come to seem more solidly grounded than in fact they are. Somewhere, midway in wandering, there comes a point when it becomes strangely difficult not to make the absurd mistake of believing that one is standing, at last, on the right path.

Reference Matter

Notes

Introduction

1. "La scienza della vita o della creazione è colta ne' suoi tratti essenziali e rappresentata con perfetta chiarezza e coesione. L'armonia intellettuale diviene cosa viva nell'architettura, così coerente e significativa nelle grandi linee, così accurata ne' minimi particolari." Francesco De Sanctis, *Storia della letteratura italiana* (Naples: Morano, 1905), p. 263; trans. Joan Redfern, *History of Italian Literature* (New York: Basic Books, 1960), p. 265.

2. Ernst Curtius, *European Literature and the Latin Middle Ages* (Princeton: Princeton University Press, 1973), p. 379. (Originally published as *Europaische Literatur und lateinisches Mittelalter* [Bern: Francke, 1948]).

Chapter One

1. "The interpretation of the *Vita Nuova* depends on knowing what portions are to be taken first and what portions are to be taken last. . . . The central canzone, which is 'Donna pietosa,' is the head of the skein, and from that point must the interpretation begin; then one must take, on this side and on that the four lateral sonnets to the left and to the right. . . . On this side and on that follow the two canzoni, placed symmetrically. . . . And thus collating the ten compositions to the right with the ten to the left, we come finally to the first and the last sonnets of the *Vita Nuova*. . . . The central part, which constitutes the Beatrice Nine, consists of nine compositions." *Gabriele Rossetti: A Versified Autobiography*, trans. and supp. William Michael Rossetti (London: Sands, 1901), p. 137; also in Kenneth McKenzie, "The Symmetrical Structure of Dante's *Vita nuova*," *Publications of the Modern*

Language Association 18 (1903): 342. Rossetti's description differs from the pattern sketched here in the text insofar as it encompasses 33 rather than 31 poems. Following the advice of his friend Charles Lyell, Rossetti includes a sonnet by Cavalcanti, and he counts as a poem the first unfinished version of "Era venuta." The 31-poem version of the pattern was "discovered" independently in 1859 by Charles Norton. For the circumstances of the pattern's original discovery, see E. R. Vincent, *Gabriele Rossetti in England* (Oxford: Clarendon Press, 1936), pp. 72–110.

2. Among the more vitriolic opponents of the hidden pattern is Michele Scherillo; see "La forma architettonica della *Vita nuova*," *Giornale dantesco* 9 (1902): 84–88. The objections of Scherillo and other Italian critics were answered by McKenzie, whose rhetoric was no less fiery: "He [Scherillo] declares that anyone who believes that Dante had the intention of arranging the *Vita Nuova* symmetrically shows 'deplorable ingenuousness and lack of critical training.' It seems to me, however, that these deplorable qualities are shown rather by attempting to deny what is evident." "Symmetrical Structure," p. 349. For the history of the pattern's initial reception, see McKenzie's article and Angelina La Piana, *Dante's American Pilgrimage* (New Haven: Yale University Press, 1948), pp. 119–21. Recent American critics of the *Vita nuova* have, by and large, accepted the pattern's deliberateness and sought to interpret it. See, for example, Charles Singleton, *An Essay on the "Vita Nuova"* (Cambridge, Mass.: Harvard University Press, 1949; reprint, Baltimore: The Johns Hopkins University Press, 1977); Mark Musa, "An Essay on the *Vita Nuova*," in *Dante's "Vita Nuova"*, ed. and trans. Mark Musa (Bloomington: University of Indiana Press, 1973); and Jerome Mazzaro, *The Figure of Dante: An Essay on the "Vita Nuova"* (Princeton: Princeton University Press, 1981). One notable exception to this trend is Robert Harrison's *The Body of Beatrice* (Baltimore: The Johns Hopkins University Press, 1988), a work to which this chapter is much indebted.

3. Singleton, *Essay*, p. 50.

4. Singleton argues that even the numerical grouping of the poems has a meaning. The pattern (viewed correctly) is engineered to reveal the Beatricean nine:

$$10 - 1 - 4 - 1 - 4 - 1 - 10$$
$$(1 + 9) - 1 - (4 + 1 + 4) - 1 - (9 + 1)$$
$$1 - 9 - 1 - 9 - 1 - 9 - 1.$$

"Here on the surface are ripples and eddies which are so many signs.
. . . signs that Beatrice is a miracle, that she is herself a number nine
which, like miracles, is the product of three times three" (ibid., pp.
79–80).

5. See, for example, Giuseppe Mazzotta's analysis of the parallels
among *Inferno* 7, *Purgatorio* 7, and *Paradiso* 7 in *Dante, Poet of the Desert* (Princeton: Princeton University Press, 1979), pp. 319–28. For a
discussion of proportional numerology, see Thomas Elwood Hart,
"The Cristo-Rhymes and Polyvalence," *Dante Studies* 105 (1987): 1–
42. For a more local kind of numerical pun on perfection, closure,
and the number 10, see R. A. Shoaf, "*Purgatorio* and *Pearl*: Transgression and Transcendence," *Texas Studies in Literature and Language* 32,
1 (1990): 155.

6. Singleton, "The Poet's Number at the Center," *Modern Language Notes* 80 (1965): 1–10. Since 1965 the hunting and debunking
of centers has become a minor cottage industry among Dante scholars (this writer included). Singleton's discovery was first attacked by
Richard Pegis in "Numerology and Probability in Dante," *Medieval
Studies* 29 (1967): 370–73. It was then defended by J. L. Logan, who
extends the pattern also to the *Purgatorio* and *Paradiso* by invoking a
principle of "mystic" addition (i.e., 142 = 1 + 4 + 2 = 7). "The Poet's
Central Numbers," *Modern Language Notes* 86 (1971): 95–98. Jeffrey
Schnapp uses slightly different arguments to find a more local center
associated with the celestial cross described in *Paradiso* 16 in *The
Transfiguration of History at the Center of Dante's "Paradise"* (Princeton: Princeton University Press, 1986), pp. 72–76, 158–59. Line
numbers are very rarely indicated on medieval manuscripts, and there
is no obvious reason why Dante should have expected his readers to
go to the trouble of counting lines for themselves; the pattern would
thus have seemed even more subtle to Dante's contemporaries than
it does to modern readers. Singleton explains this puzzle by suggesting that Dante, like other medieval artists, composed his patterns to
please God rather than man: "We know that such an edifice [Chartres]
was not addressed to human sight alone, indeed not primarily to human sight at all. He who sees all things and so marvelously created
the world in number, weight, and measure, would see that design, no
matter where its place in the structure." "Poet's Number," p. 10.

7. In order to make the pattern work, one must not count the unfinished version of "Era venuta" as a poem at all. One must classify

the unfinished canzone "Quantunque volte" as a non-canzone. And, most questionable of all, one must classify the unfinished canzone "Sì lungiamente" as a sonnet. This final point is taken up at greater length later in this chapter.

8. Charles Singleton, ed. and trans., *The Divine Comedy*, vol. 3, *Paradiso* (Princeton: Princeton University Press, 1975), p. 609.

9. Harrison, *Body of Beatrice*, p. 11.

10. One critic who suggests that truncation is managed for poetic effect is Nancy J. Vickers: "The act of writing is interrupted, and interruption ironically transforms, through abrupt truncation, the would-be *canzone* back into a perfectly crafted sonnet." "Widowed Words: Metaphors of Mourning," in *Discourses of Authority in Medieval and Renaissance Literature*, ed. Kevin Brownlee and Walter Stevens (Hanover, N.H.: University Press of New England, 1989), p. 99.

11. The proper category for the lyric "Sì lungiamente" is in fact the subject of some difference of opinion among critics. Kenelm Foster and Patrick Boyde, in *Dante's Lyric Poetry*, (London: Oxford University Press, 1967), 2: 129, summarize the points for and against its classification as a sonnet: "It has the necessary fourteen lines (in itself, not significant); the *pedes* correspond exactly to those of a sonnet (unique among canzone-stanzas by stilnovisti . . .), there is no *verso chiave* (unique in Dante's canzoni, but quite common—e.g., in Cino). The differences are that 1.11 is a heptasyllable, and even if it were not (assuming that *chiamando* remained in rhyme), the resultant rhyme scheme—CDD; CEE—never occurs in any of Dante's sonnets where each *volta* always contains all the rhymes." Foster and Boyde classify the poem as a canzone-stanza, but they note the irony of Dante's presentation of his work as a fragment that is not a sonnet. "What is interesting and even amusing is that Dante protests in the prose that he did not think he could treat his subject 'in brevitade di sonetto' whereas not only is the stanza self-contained in its fourteen lines, but the theme is stated in full in the first four." Ultimately it is not so much a question of whether "Sì lungiamente" "really" is a sonnet, but whether the play between perfection and imperfection is significant.

12. The structure of the prose is briefly discussed in Singleton's *Essay*. Singleton claims that since "Donna pietosa" is "contained in chapter twenty-three, and since the last chapter of the *Vita Nuova* is numbered forty-two, the death of Beatrice could hardly be more centrally placed" (p. 7). But as Harrison points out, 42 divided in half

does not equal 23. The chapter containing "Donna pietosa" comes *close* to the numerical center of the prose chapters, but it does not come *at* the center. The prose "center" that I will be discussing is determined not numerically, but by the chapters' varying form.

13. Oddly enough, the *Comedy* presents much the same problem. In a 1954 essay, Singleton claims that Beatrice's return in the procession in Earthly Paradise (canto 30) takes place at the center of the *Comedy*—a return that mirrors Beatrice's disappearance in the *Vita nuova*: "In the *Vita Nuova*, at the center of the *Vita Nuova*, Beatrice is seen to depart from this life. . . . At the *center* of the *Divine Comedy*, Beatrice comes, Beatrice returns." "Pattern at the Center," in *Elements of Structure*, ed. Charles Singleton (Cambridge, Mass.: Harvard University Press, 1954), p. 57 (emphasis mine). In 1965, Singleton contradicts this claim with marvelous confidence (or perhaps self-irony?); in the lead sentence to "Poet's Number," Singleton blithely announces that "the central canto of the *Commedia* is, *of course*, the seventeenth of the *Purgatorio*, the central *cantica*" (emphasis mine). How can the center of the *Comedy* be located in *Purgatorio* 30 and also in *Purgatorio* 17?

14. See Harrison, *Body of Beatrice*, chaps. 6 and 7.

Chapter Two

1. Charles Singleton, ed. and trans., *The Divine Comedy*, vol. 1; *Inferno* (Princeton: Princeton University Press, 1970), pp. 43–44, 312; Dorothy Sayers, ed. and trans., *The Divine Comedy: Hell* (Harmondsworth, Eng.: Penguin Books, 1958), p. 138; Carlo Salinari, Sergio Romagnoli, and Antonio Lanza, eds., *La Divina Commedia: Inferno* (Rome: Riuniti, 1980), p. xxxii.

2. The first commentary to include a numerical calculation of the dimensions of the infernal terrain is the early-fourteenth-century *Ottimo commento*, 3 vols. (Pisa: Niccolò Capurro, 1827–29). The author of *L'Ottimo* extrapolates from Dante's measurements of the ninth and tenth ditches of the Malebolge to determine the dimensions of the eight ditches that Dante does not explicitly measure. For a discussion of fourteenth-century representations of the infernal terrain, see Peter Brieger, "Pictorial Commentaries to the *Commedia*," in *Illuminated Manuscripts of the "Divine Comedy"*, ed. Peter Brieger, Millard Meiss, and Charles S. Singleton, (Princeton: Princeton University Press, 1969), 1: 98–99.

3. Vasari, *Le vite de' più eccellenti pittori scultori ed architettori* (Florence: Batteli, 1848), p. 685.

4. Some of the calculations are also recorded in the marginal notes and diagrams that accompany an edition of the *Commedia* copied in Manetti's hand located in the Biblioteca Nazionale. Manetti was also friendly with Brunelleschi—a friendship recorded in comic detail in Manetti's novella, *Il grasso legnaiuolo*, and reflected more seriously in Manetti's *Vita di Filippo Brunelleschi*.

5. Most of the editions date from the last decades of the fifteenth century, but the commentary was still popular enough to be reproduced as late as 1596.

6. Benivieni's "dialogo circa el sito forma et misure dello Inferno" accompanied his 1506 edition of the *Comedy*. Edited versions of the *dialogo* were also published in 1855 and 1897 by Ottavo Gigli, *Studi sulla Divina Commedia* (Florence: Felice, 1855), pp. 37–132, and by Zingarelli. Alessandro Vellutello's "descrittione de lo Inferno" was published along with his 1544 commentary. Francesco Giambullari's "De 'l sito forma e misure dell' Inferno" also dates from 1544. For a discussion of the other critical works produced by these cartographers, see Aldo Vallone, *L'interpretazione di Dante nel cinquecento* (Florence: Leo S. Olschki, 1969).

7. In several editions, the maps are explicitly advertised on the title page: "Dante col sito et forma dell'inferno tratta dalla istessa descrittione del poeta" (1515); "Dante col sito, et forma dell' inferno" (1515, 1516, 1520).

8. As opposed to Landino, who argues that Hell stretches the full distance from the earth's center to its edge—a distance he set at 3,400 miles—Vellutello argues that Hell is much smaller—a cavity only 315 miles deep. Nor is Vellutello the only cartographer to differ with Manetti and his followers. In his "De 'l sito forma e misure dell' Inferno," Francesco Giambullari insists that the well containing Cocytus is only as deep as the giant Antaeus can reach, whereas Benivieni argues that it is considerably deeper. Almost every cartographer offers a different estimate of the heights of Satan, Nimrod, and the other giants. Indeed, the only features of the infernal terrain that the Renaissance cartographers consistently agree upon are the dimensions of the pits of the Malebolge. But even those calculations differ quite sharply from the calculations of the fourteenth-century commentators.

9. Misplaced in the files of the Biblioteca Nazionale in Florence, these lectures, written in Galileo's own hand, were rescued from oblivion by Ottavo Gigli in 1855. They were subsequently republished by E. Mestica in 1889, and more recently by Alberto Chiari: "Galileo Galilei, Due lezioni all'Accademia Fiorentina circa la figura, sito e grandezza dell'inferno di Dante," in *Scritti litterari* (Florence: Felice Le Monnier, 1943), pp. 47–80. All subsequent citations of Galileo's lectures are from Chiari's edition of the "Lezioni."

10. "Mirabilmente, dunque, possiamo concludere aver investigata il Manetti la mente del nostro Poeta." Galileo, "Lezioni," p. 59.

11. Writing of Landino, "S'ingegnò di voler intendere e manifestar questa verità, ma invano, havendo 'l cieco preso per sua guida."

12. Chiari goes as far as suggesting that Galileo's calculations were intended as a means of winning a professorship from his flattered audience.

13. See J. B. Harley and David Woodward, *The History of Cartography* (Chicago: University of Chicago Press, 1987); Norman Thrower, *Maps and Man* (Englewood Cliffs, N.J.: Prentice-Hall, 1972), pp. 43–55. There were accurate maps already in circulation in the fourteenth century, but these were sea charts rather than comprehensive atlases.

14. Among the works that Manetti copied in his own hand and that survive in the Biblioteca Nazionale are a pair of geographical treatises—*Imago mundi* and *Della imagine del mondo di Santo Isidero*. Manetti also corresponded with Pozzo Toscanelli, a mathematician and physician who played an essential role in arranging for Columbus's voyages. See Robert and Valerie Martone's introduction to their translation of Manetti's *Il grasso legnaiuolo* (New York: Italica Press, 1991), p. xiii.

15. Alessandro Parronchi specifically argues that there is a connection between the rise of infernal cartography and the rising importance of perspective in Renaissance art. "La perspettiva dantesca," *Studi danteschi* 36 (1958–59): 9–11.

16. Galileo, *Dialogo dei massimi sistemi* (1632), dedication. The translation is from Galileo, *Dialogue Concerning the Two Chief World Systems*, trans. Stillman Drake (Berkeley: University of California Press, 1967), p. 3.

17. See Ernst Curtius, *European Literature and the Latin Middle Ages* (Princeton: Princeton University Press, 1973), entries on "The Book of Nature," pp. 319–26, and "Numerical Composition," pp. 501–10.

For a general discussion of the role of ratio and proportion in medieval cosmology, see Leo Spitzer, *Classical and Christian Ideas of World Harmony—Prolegomena to an Interpretation of the Word "Stimmung"* (Baltimore: The Johns Hopkins University Press, 1963). It is worth remembering that although Renaissance readers may have been more persistent in their efforts to map Hell, there were also fourteenth-century commentators who studied Hell's proportions with great care—most notably L' Ottimo, but also Benvenuto and Guido da Pisa.

18.   When Dante defines beauty in the *Convivio*, for example, it is as a correspondence of parts, "Quella cosa dice l'uomo essere bella, cui le parti debitamente si rispondono, per che de la loro armonia resulta piacimento. . . ." *Convivio*, ed., Cesare Vasoli and Domenico De Robertis (Naples: Riccardo Ricciardi, 1988), 1.5.13. In the *Paradiso*, Dante discusses the "order" that makes the universe resemble God: "Le cose tutte quante / hanno ordine tra loro, e questo è forma / che l'universo a Dio fa simigliante" (*Par.* 1.103–5). Dante's sense of number, ratio, and proportion is discussed at length in J. F. Took, *"L'etterno piacer": Aesthetic Ideas in Dante* (Oxford: Clarendon Press, 1984). In assessing the role of number in the *Comedy*, it is necessary to distinguish between two branches of medieval numerology: the branch devoted to uncovering allegorical correspondences and the branch devoted to displaying abstract symmetries and structures. These two forms of numerology are often pursued simultaneously by medieval authors (Dante included), but they are in fact quite different in spirit and origin. Whereas allegorical numerology borders on cryptography, the second, more abstract form of numerology borders on science and aesthetics. The sapiential formula, "Sed omnia in mensura, et numero, et pondere disposuisti," is clearly inscribed within the second tradition. It is in this tradition that I am locating Dante's measurements of the terrain.

19.   This is the calculation that one finds in *L'Ottimo commento*: "Pare che l'Autore voglia mettere ciascuna bolgia due cotanti in giro l'una che l'altra . . . se la decima bolgia è undici miglia in circumferenza, la nona è ventidue, la ottava è quaranta quattro ec.; e qui usa geometria" (p. 496). Renaissance and nineteenth-century cartographers opted instead for an arithmetic series—11, 22, 33, etc. They did so because, as was already observed in the fourteenth century, the scheme of L'Ottimo would make the Malebolge too large to be easily accommodated in a map of Hell; at the rate suggested by L'Ottimo, the Ma-

lebolge would be 5,632 miles in circumference and have a diameter of 1,792 miles.

20. Grandgent makes this point in his commentary but nevertheless insists that calculation and extrapolation are the wrong responses to Dante's measurements. C. Grandgent, *La Divina Commedia* (Boston: Heath, 1933), p. 233.

21. The Archimedean value $^{22}/_{7}$ was the most accurate and most commonly used estimate of *pi* from the classical period through the Renaissance. It appears in texts as diverse as Macrobius's commentary on the *Somnium Scipionis* and primers on practical arithmetic like Piero della Francesca's *De abaco*. For a general survey, see Peter Beckmann, *A History of Pi* (Boulder, Colo.: Golem Press, 1977).

22. Macrobius, *Commentary on the Dream of Scipio*, trans. William Stahl (New York: Columbia University Press, 1952), p. 171.

23. One method is to assume that when Dante describes a point on the earth's surface, he is, at that moment, directly below it. The most common method, however, is simply to continue to extrapolate on the basis of some arbitrarily imposed schema. Some critics, like Giambullari, even extended their calculations to include Purgatory ("Del sito del purgatorio," 1541). The insensitivity of Renaissance critics to the deliberate obscurity of the opening cantos is most apparent in Benivieni's attempt to fix the place of the dark wood on the map of Italy: "La selva è, o la finge esser, tra monte Miseno e Cuma, circa a Pozzuolo in su la marina." Gigli, ed., *Studi*, p. 52.

24. When Dante and Virgil laboriously invert their bodies on Satan's flank, they perform an act of symbolic conversion that also provides a precise definition of their location—their inversion could only be performed at the dead center of the earth. As the travelers pass through the center of the earth, the direction of gravity changes abruptly. What was the downward direction becomes the upward direction, and to continue to move forward they must invert their bodies. The end of the descent is thus the single moment in the poem when we can say with complete confidence where the two travelers are located.

25. Between 1750 and 1820 at least seven editions were accompanied by mathematically exacting maps attributed to Manetti. In a Venetian edition of 1778, for example, the illustration of Hell is explicitly identified as: "PROFILO, PIANTA, E MISURE DELL'INFERNO DI DANTE SECONDO LA DESCRIZIONE *d'Antonio Manetti Fiorentino*."

26. Vaccheri and Bertacchi's *La visione di Dante Allighieri considerata nel tempo e nello spazio* (Turin: Editrice Candeletti, 1881) is the most innovative of all the studies of the shape of Hell, arguing that Dante begins his journey at the base of Purgatory rather than the opposite side of the earth. This shift of the origin necessitates the complete rejection of the conical model of Hell. Michelangeli's *Sul disegno dell'Inferno dantesco* (Bologna: Nicola Zanichelli, 1886) is less astonishingly original but does propose a remarkable model of the Malebolge. In an effort to produce a map that respects the complicated gravitational field near the center of the earth, Michelangeli sketches a Malebolge that looks more like a profile of the Andes than a set of moats and bridges.

27. For a summary, albeit a biased one, of nineteenth-century speculations, see Giovanni Agnelli, *Topo-cronografia del viaggio dantesco* (Milan: Hoepli, 1891). Typical of the debate is the series of four polemical articles exchanged in the *Giornale dantesco* between Agnelli and Zingarelli over the presence or absence of a steep slope between the fifth and sixth circles. The series begins with Zingarelli's "Il sesto cerchio nella topografia dell' *Inferno*," *Giornale dantesco* 4 (1897): 194–218, to which Agnelli responds with "Tra il quinto e il sesto cerchio dell' *Inferno*," *Giornale dantesco* 5 (1898): 117–25. Zingarelli responds to Agnelli's criticism in "Polemica," *Giornale dantesco* 5 (1898): 474–76, and Agnelli replies in "Ancora tra il quinto e sesto cerchio dell' *Inferno* dantesco," *Giornale dantesco* 6 (1898): 396–402.

28. Enzo Esposito, *Lectura Dantis* (Rome, 1931): "C'è un angolo appartato della dantologia tenuto tutto di cosidetti misuratori, patetiche figure di studiosi che spendono tempo ed energie in calcoli tanto pazienti quanto poco utilizzabili in ordine alla valutazione estetica."

29. "The great, authentic trunk of early Dante studies." Umberto Bosco and Giovanni Reggio, eds., *La Divina Commedia* (Florence: Le Monnier, 1978), 1: 459.

30. Bosco and Reggio assert, "Ma, come per le misure dei cerchi . . . non si debbono trarre conseguenze precise: Dante le dà solo per rendere più *reale* il suo viaggio, per dargli una *parvenza* di cosa concreta. Sifatti calcoli sono frutto di critica oziosa che tratta le ombre come cosa salda" (ibid., p. 459, emphasis mine). In the entry on "miglio" in the *Enciclopedia Dantesca*, one finds the following assessment

of Dante's use of distances: "Nella *Commedia miglio* indica, innanzi-
tutto, le misure del mondo infernale, intese non già a un'effettiva,
impossibile misurazione, ma a dare al lettore un'impressione di mas-
sima concretezza." (*Enciclopedia Dantesca*, dir. Umberto Bosco, ed.
Giorgio Petrocchi (Rome, 1970–78), 3:952. The distance "22 miles"
is not to be taken as a literal measurement: "E ovvio che l'indicazione
non va presa alla lettera, trattandosi di 'parole poetiche'" (5: 943). In
analyzing the same passages, Grandgent observes, "These figures do
not afford a clue for any further computations; they give, however,
an impression of exactness" *Divina Commedia*, p. 258. Singleton makes
a similar point about the "realism" of the measurements but does ex-
hibit some curiosity concerning their limited accuracy: "Such precise
measurements are calculated to add realism to the description of Hell,
but they in fact show a curious indifference to reality." *Divine Come-
dy*, 1: 558. An alternative explanation has recently been proposed by
Victoria Kirkham in "Eleven Is for Evil: Measured Trespass in Dante's
Commedia," *Allegorica* 10 (1989): 27–50. Kirkham argues for a nu-
merological reading based on the symbolic significance of the num-
ber eleven. A very similar reading of the measurements is proposed
by Vincent Hopper, who notes, "Eleven is the number of sin since
the time of Augustine." *Medieval Number Symbolism* (New York: Cor-
nell University Press, 1938), p. 152.

31. Sayers, ed. and trans., *Divine Comedy: Hell*, pp. 350–51.

32. This temporal reference is contained in the same passage in
which the dimensions of the ninth *bolgia* are given. Virgil announces,
"Pensa, se tu annoverar le credi, / che miglia ventidue la valle volge. /
E già la luna è sotto i nostri piedi" (*Inf.* 29.8–10). Remarkably, the
very same commentators who dismiss the spatial measurement are
willing to treat the more obscure astronomical image as an important
indication of the journey's chronology. See, for example, Grand-
gent's and Bosco's comments on *Inf.* 29.9 in Grandgent, *Divina
Commedia*, p. 233, and Bosco and Reggio, eds., *Divina Commedia*
1:428.

33. Critics have admitted some uncertainty about the height of the
giants. The lowest estimates approach 50 feet, the highest 100 feet.

34. Note Manetti's warning in Landino's cartographic preface:
"Bisognerebbe lasciare indietro i Giganti e Lucifero perché guaster-
ebbero ogni cosa."

35. Assuming the *central* radius of the tenth ditch is $1\frac{3}{4}$ miles, we can infer that the inner edge of the tenth ditch should be $1\frac{1}{2}$ miles from the central axis of Hell.

36. The size of the giant bronze pine-cone, which is currently located in the papal palace, was much debated. Vellutello and Landino worried over whether it had been taller in Dante's time than it was in the sixteenth century. Currently the pine-cone stands over twelve feet tall; if it was taller in Dante's time, the discrepancy between head and body would be even greater. The size of the Frieslanders is also subject to some speculation. There is no way to know exactly how tall a Frieslander was in Dante's imagination or in the imagination of his readers. The Frieslanders enjoyed the reputation of an unusually tall people, but there is no evidence to suggest that they were imagined as twelve-foot-tall giants.

37. Peter Dronke, *Dante and Medieval Latin Traditions* (Cambridge: Cambridge University Press, 1986), pp. 37–43.

38. The depth of the well is a much-contested point. Most cartographers invoke Dante's observation in canto 32, "Come noi fummo giù nel pozzo scuro / sotto i piè del gigante assai più bassi," to argue that the pit is deeper than Antaeus's reach; others, such as the Renaissance critic Francesco Giambullari, argue that this would contradict Dante's own description of his descent (*Inf.* 32.16–17). Giambullari's argument runs as follows: when Antaeus picks up the travelers, they are standing at the edge of the central well; when Antaeus releases them, they are standing at the base of the well; therefore, the well must be roughly half the height of the giant.

Grandgent's attempt to explain the pit's depth provides excellent evidence of how far one must strain in order to fit Dante's various references together. Grandgent suggests that since Antaeus is unbound by any chains, he is free to move about and therefore can climb down the slope of Hell before bending over to deposit the travelers on the surface of Cocytus. I quote from his commentary: "Antaeus, therefore, carrying the poets, must have left his place and climbed down the precipice; but of this descent our author, for reasons of his own, says not a word. Perhaps he conceived of himself as so terrified that he could recall nothing of the adventure but its awful beginning and end." *Divina Commedia*, p. 274. There are a few critics who admit that there is a contradiction: "There seems to be a contradiction here, comparable to that implied in the measure of 'half a mile across' given for the tenth *bolgia*." Singleton, *Divine Comedy*, 1: 580. Dorothy Sayers writes about the problem with the central pit in a private letter to the mapmaker for her Penguin translation of the *Inferno*, "Ah, yes, now we really are up against trouble, and not (I fear) of our making. Dante has been naughty, and made an inconsistency, hoping that nobody would notice." Cited in Barbara Reynolds, *The Passionate Intellect: Dorothy L. Sayers' Encounter with Dante* (Kent, Ohio: Kent State University Press, 1989), p. 77.

39. John Freccero's interpretation of the writing on the gates of Hell provides an excellent model for making sense of mismeasurement. Emphasizing the disquieting context of the *Inferno*'s "realism," Freccero argues that the "realism" so often praised by Dante's critics is, for Dante, an essentially ironic mode, at least within the first cantica. "Infernal Irony: The Gates of Hell," in *Dante: The Poetics of Conversion*, ed. Rachel Jacoff (Cambridge, Mass.: Harvard University Press, 1986), pp. 93–109.

40. The cantos of Fraud are not, however, the only section of the *Inferno* to include scenes of elusive order. Two earlier examples are the notoriously difficult passages in *Inferno* 11 and 14 where Virgil explains Hell's moral system and its complex system of rivers, lakes, and canals. These passages seem, at first glance, to express a pedantic taste for elaborately defined structures; they are so extensive and so undramatic that their function seems only one of clarification. Yet anyone who has spent time with these passages knows that they provide only a semblance of order—when closely examined, the order they promise proves to be irresolvably problematic. This has, over the years, caused some consternation among critics, yet in both cases the troubles could be deliberate. The moral system of Hell is unfolded within the single circle whose position in the system is most problematic; though Virgil and Dante are standing among the heretics, Virgil never explains how heresy is to be accommodated within Aristotelian categories. The discourse on the hydraulic system of Hell is, one could argue, similarly incongruous. Following closely upon the magical allegory of the Old Man of Crete, it comes to seem by its context comically pragmatic; Dante has been regaled with a fabulous account of a huge, blood-weeping statue, yet all he wants to know is how the rivers flow.

41. *De vulgari* 1.7.4, in *Opere Minori*, ed. G. Squarotti and S. Cecchin (Turin: UTET, 1983). The translation is from R. Haller, *Literary*

Criticism of Dante Alighieri (Lincoln: University of Nebraska Press, 1973), p. 10.

42. Like Nimrod's tower, the enormous bronze cone is a work that pits the human artist against God. God's humble work—the pine-cone—is set against a huge, glorious, and excessive sculpture. Marianne Moore makes much the same point when she describes the same bronze pine-cone in her poem "Too Much . . .".

43. Hugh Libergier (d. 1263), the builder of St. Nicaise, appears in Reims Cathedral clasping a miniature church while at his feet are propped a square and compass; reproduced in Otto von Simson, *The Gothic Cathedral* (Princeton: Princeton University Press, 1974), fig. 6b. For a similar use of the compass, see the c. 1250 manuscript reproduced in John Murdoch, *Album of Science: Antiquity and the Middle Ages* (New York: Charles Scribner's Sons, 1984), p. 209.

44. Robert Harrison first directed my attention to the two complementary analogies between proportion and justice and between disproportion and injustice.

45. *Poetics*, chap. 21.

46. For Nimrod's short line, see Hopper, *Medieval Number Symbolism*, p. 153. I have Elizabeth Statmore to thank for advising me that Adamo's *rima composta* might be significant in the context of Dante's mismeasurements. There are nine examples of *rima composta* in the *Comedy*; Adamo's rhyme is, however, the only example to combine three words. See Alfonso de Salvio, *The Rhyme Words in the Divine Comedy* (Paris: Librairie Ancienne, 1929), p. 113.

47. As Dante observes in the *Convivio*, "L'ordine debito de le nostre membra rende uno piacere non so di che armonia mirabile" (*Conv.* 4.25.12). This formula is part of a long tradition; citing Dionysius, Aquinas explains that the human body is beautiful because it exhibits the "universorum consonantiae" of the cosmos in its "membra bene proportionata." Alanus ab Insulis argues that man is an image of the cosmos because he is a tempering of differences into a single consonant whole. See Spitzer, *Classical and Christian Ideas*, p. 73.

48. *Quaestiones disputatae de veritate* 23.6 (Rome: Marietti, 1949).

49. *Ethics* 5.3–6, in *The Basic Works of Aristotle*, ed. Richard McKeon (New York: Random House, 1941).

50. Ibid., 5.4.4.

51. The term *contrapasso* comes from the section of the *Ethics* that deals with the proportions of Justice: book 5, chap. 5. *Contrapasso*

appears as the last word of canto 28 and the first measurement appears at the start of canto 29.

Chapter Three

1. The fresco is located in the cathedral at Orvieto. Scenes of reading are in fact standard elements in the early portraits of Dante. In Vasari's group portrait of the trecento poets, Dante is shown reading from a book entitled "Virgil." On the 1483 tomb at Ravenna, Pietro Lombardi depicts the poet in the act of comparing manuscripts. See Richard Holbrook, *Portraits of Dante from Giotto to Raffael* (London: Philip Lee Warner, 1909).

2. *Trattatello in laude di Dante* (1351).

3. Giovanni del Virgilio, epitaph for Dante's tomb (1321); Giovanni Villani, *Cronica* (1348); Leonardo Bruni, *Dialogi ad Petrum Paulum histrum* (1436).

4. The Dartmouth Dante project provides fine evidence of the tradition's strength: in this case, Dante scholars have moved into the computer age by putting medieval and Renaissance commentaries on a hard drive.

5. Misreading is, for example, a major theme in Teodolinda Barolini's comprehensive study, *Dante's Poets: Textuality and Truth in the Comedy* (Princeton: Princeton University Press, 1984). For more recent explorations of the topic, see the essays by Brownlee, Hawkins, Jacoff, Schnapp, and Stephany in *The Poetry of Allusion: Virgil and Ovid in Dante's Commedia*, ed. Rachel Jacoff and Jeffrey Schnapp (Stanford: Stanford University Press, 1991).

6. In fact, it is not clear in the *Thebaid* whether the common soldiers even see their general's departure. Though Statius describes the soldiers' amazement at the shuddering of the earth (7.794), nowhere does he explicitly indicate that they actually witness Amphiaraus's disappearance. Indeed, after Amphiaraus has disappeared, they are shown searching the field for his body and chariot (8.127).

7. *Met.* 3.316–41.

8. This position is clearly articulated in the entry on "Classica Cultura" by Manlio Pastore Stocchi in the *Enciclopedia Dantesca* and in the individual entries on "Euripilo," "Manto," and "Aronta." *Enciclopedia Dantesca*, dir. Umberto Bosco, ed. Giorgio Petrocchi, 5 vols. plus app. (Rome, 1970–78). A masterful example of this kind of textual study is that of Fausto Ghisalberti on the confusion between

Oedipus and the water nymphs, "L'enigma delle Naiadi," *Studi danteschi* 16 (1932): 105–25.

9. "Aronta" (Giorgio Padoan) and "Euripilo" (Carla Kraus) entries in the *Enciclopedia Dantesca*. Facing the problem of Arruns's misplaced home, Padoan responds as follows: "Meno facilmente spiegabile (ma probabilmente pur sempre riconducibile a lezione particolare del codice usato dal poeta) è il passaggio dai 'moenia' ai *monti*" (1: 388). After reviewing possible explanations concerning Manto's misplacement, Padoan makes the claim, "Non rimane che ipotizzare un errore testuale" (3:811).

10. Hollander, "The Tragedy of Divination," in *Studies in Dante* (Ravenna: Longo, 1980), pp. 131–218. A much-revised version of this essay appears in *Poetry of Allusion*, ed. Jacoff and Schnapp, pp. 77–93, under the title "Dante's Misreadings of the *Aeneid* in *Inferno* 20."

11. "Classica Cultura" entry in the *Enciclopedia Dantesca*.

12. There are other examples of this technique to be found outside *Inferno* 20. Dronke has noted, for example, the comic impropriety of Dante's not quite classic classical giants. Peter Dronke, *Dante and Medieval Latin Traditions* (Cambridge: Cambridge University Press, 1986). Biow has explored the disquieting effect of learned allusion in *Inferno* 13. Douglas Biow, "From Ignorance to Knowledge: The Marvelous in *Inferno* 13," in *The Poetry of Allusion: Virgil and Ovid in Dante's Commedia*, ed. Rachel Jacoff and Jeffrey Schnapp (Stanford: Stanford University Press, 1991).

13. In the *Aeneid*, Eurypylus is named solely by Sinon; the brief references in the *Iliad* to Eurypylus would not have been known to Dante.

14. It is occasionally suggested that Dante's handling of Manto is influenced by Isidore, Servius, or Statius. Such efforts to trace the problem to conflicting source-texts are not very convincing because it is clear that Virgil is taking his own text as a point of reference. The *Aeneid* is the first (and most important) text to find a mythological origin for Mantua.

15. The same basic pattern is discernible in the encounters with Pier della Vigna and Geryon. As Dante stresses the truth of his account in contradistinction to lying fictions, one inevitably wonders how Dante's poem can be different.

16. Not every critic can, of course, be so easily categorized. Giu-

seppe Mazzotta, for example, presents a portrait of a more anxious poet, a portrait that influences his comments about *Inferno* 20 in *Dante, Poet of the Desert* (Princeton: Princeton University Press, 1979), p. 318.

17. This canto has been closely considered in broad studies such as Hollander's *Allegory in Dante's "Commedia"* (Princeton: Princeton University Press, 1969) and Barolini's *Dante's Poets*. For specific investigations of the canto, see, for example, Christopher Kleinhenz, "The Celebration of Poetry: A Reading of *Purgatorio* XXII," *Dante Studies* 106 (1988): 21–42. See also Ronald Martinez, "La *sacra fame dell'oro* (*Purgatorio* 22.41) tra Virgil e Stazio: dal testo all'interpretazione," *Letture classensi* 18 (1989): 177–93. R. A. Shoaf, "'Auri sacra fames' and the Age of Gold," *Dante Studies* 96 (1978): 195–99.

18. In Petrocchi's edition of the *Comedy*, line 40 begins "Per che non reggi tu," not "Perché non reggi tu."

19. That the Virgilian line is itself ambiguous when taken out of context has, perhaps, helped shape Dante's choice of allusion: the duality of the line conveniently mimics the duality of punishments on the terrace of Avarice/Prodigality.

20. Niccoli, speaking in a dialogue composed by Bruni in 1401, has the following harsh words for Dante: "Do we not often see him erring in such a way that he seems to have been utterly ignorant? He very obviously did not know what was meant by those words of Virgil's, 'To what do you not drive mortal hearts, accursed hunger for gold?'—which words have never been doubtful to anyone of even moderate learning." Cited in *Dante: The Critical Heritage*, ed. Michael Caesar (London: Routledge, 1989), p. 191.

21. The desire to excuse or obscure Dante's apparent mistake is especially apparent in the work of his translators. Given a choice between rendering Dante's Italian correctly and thus revealing his error or providing a protective mistranslation, most English translators have taken the latter path. The group includes Cary, Longfellow, Norton, Sinclair, Singleton, and Musa.

22. "How could it happen that he who saw through to Virgil's most obscure meanings should be led astray by this obvious verse? It is not so: either it is the fault of the scribes (most of whom are ignorant dolts), or Virgil's saying has been applied to the other extreme" (1401). Cited in *Critical Heritage*, ed. Caesar, p. 194.

23. See Natalino Sapegno, *La Divina Commedia*, 2d ed. (Florence: La Nuova Italia, 1968), and Giorgio Petrocchi, *La Commedia*

secondo l'antica vulgata, Società Dantesca Italiana, edizione nazionale (Milan: Mondadori, 1967), 3: 373.

24. C. Grandgent, *La Divina Commedia* (Boston: Heath, 1933), p. 189.

25. See, for example, Shoaf, "Age of Gold," pp. 195–99. After citing the Augustinian command to "spoil the Egyptians," Shoaf brackets Dante's error in the following way: "His [Statius'] very 'mistranslation' of Virgil's text is eloquent testimony of Statius' conversion to the true faith. Dante's subtle metamorphosis of Virgil's text is eloquent testimony of his profound understanding of Christian hermeneutics." Hollander opts for the term "misreading" over "mistranslation." "Tragedy of Divination," pp. 212–13. Barolini avoids the prefix "mis" altogether by referring to the mistranslated passage as an instance of "changed significance." *Dante's Poets*, p. 259.

26. See Beryl Smalley, *The Study of the Bible in the Middle Ages* (Oxford: Basil Blackwell, 1952); Ann Astell, *The Song of Songs in the Middle Ages* (Ithaca, N.Y.: Cornell University Press, 1990).

27. See Domenico Comparetti, *Vergil in the Middle Ages*, trans. E. Benecke (New York: Macmillan, 1895), pp. 219–31, and R. W. Chambers, "Long Will, Dante, and the Righteous Heathen," *Essays and Studies* 9 (1923): 50–69.

28. *Introductio*, Prol., *Patrologiae Latina* (Paris: Migne, 1844–64), 178–1008B; *Exégèse* 2.2, p. 255. Cited in Winthrop Wetherbee, *Platonism and Poetry in the Twelfth Century* (Princeton: Princeton University Press, 1972), p. 40.

29. Many explanations for this apparent contradiction have been proposed over the years, most of them involving some kind of scribal blunder. They are baroque in their ingenuity, and no particular theory has ever won wide acceptance. For a survey, see the *Enciclopedia Dantesca* entry on "Manto."

30. *Cronica di Giovanni Villani*: Michael Scot (12.19–92), Guido Bonatti (7.81). Dante names Asdente (Maestro Benvenuto) in *Convivio* 6.16.6. *Convivio*, ed. Cesare Vasoli and Domenico De Robertis (Naples: Riccardo Ricciardi, 1988).

31. One apparent exception to this rule is Virgil's naming of Farinata in *Inferno* 10: "Vedi là Farinata che s'è dritto" (10.32). In fact, this naming is carefully prepared for. First, Farinata is named by Dante during his conversation with Ciacco in *Inferno* 6—Farinata is the first of the "worthy" Florentines whose fate Dante enquires about. Sec-

ond, Farinata appears within a tomb that, presumably, bears his name. When Dante and Virgil pause to discuss the order of Hell in *Inferno* 11, they approach another open tomb with a clear, legible inscription: "Ci raccostammo, in dietro, ad un coperchio / d'un grand' avello, ov'io vidi una scritta / che dicea: '*Anastasio papa guardo*'" (*Inf.* 11.6–8). There are, moreover, many points in the *Inferno* and *Purgatorio* where Virgil's actions do not make sense, if we assume that he does possess a complete knowledge of events after his lifetime. Virgil explains to Statius, for example, that he knows about his work only because of conversations with Juvenal in Limbo (*Purg.* 22.10–18).

32. I have emphasized the epistemological problem in granting Virgil knowledge of contemporary Italy, but one could just as easily stress the generic difficulty. One reason Virgil does not normally name Italian figures or comment on Italian history is his status as an exemplary classical poet. It is Dante, the modern poet, who mixes with the moderns. For Virgil, to discuss Asdente is to stoop from his lofty pose.

33. Benvenuto emphasizes the newness of the fortress: "Satis novum, munitum multis turribus et arcibus, quasi tutela totius contratae."

34. See, for example, the conversation with Statius in *Purgatorio* 22, where Virgil explains how he learned about his Toulousan admirer from the recently dead (and damned) Juvenal.

35. *Medieval Literary Theory and Criticism*, ed. Alastair Minnis and Alexander Scott, with the assistance of David Wallace (Oxford: Clarendon Press, 1988), p. 440.

36. To readers accustomed to seeing Dante as an exemplary apologist for Christian dogma, this may seem an implausible claim. Such readers may be tempted to argue that if the patterns of error are deliberate, then they must be affirmative and *not* self-critical. There are many sources that might anchor such a reading. One could, for example, turn to the eighth book of the *Confessions* and the scene of Augustine's conversion. Standing at the base of a fig tree, Augustine listens to the voices of children playing, voices Augustine acknowledges he may be misinterpreting, and then follows their command: "All at once I heard the sing-song voice of a child in a nearby house. Whether it was the voice of a boy or a girl I cannot say, but again and again it repeated the refrain 'Take it and read, take it and read.' ['Tolle lege, tolle lege.'] At this I looked up, thinking hard whether there was any kind of game in which children used to chant words like these,

but I could not remember hearing them before." Opening the Bible and again hearing its words as a command addressed directly to him, Augustine finally finds the courage to convert: "I read the first passage on which my eyes fell: 'Not in revelling and drunkness, not in quarrels and rivalries. Rather arm yourselves with the Lord Jesus Christ; spend no more thought on nature and nature's appetites.' I had no wish to read more and no need to do so." *Confessions*, trans. R. S. Pine-Coffin (London: Penguin Books, 1961), 8.12. By accepting words spoken in play as a command from God, Augustine scores a critical victory over his training in rhetoric and classical philosophy. He humbles his scholar's pride to accept a salvation mediated by misreading. It is just this type of interpretive humility that, one could argue, is at work in *Inferno* 20 and *Purgatorio* 22.

For still another defense of error, one might consult the writings of Origen. In his account of his reading method, Origen identifies the cruxes of a text as the points where the most profound meaning resides and cautions readers against blaming Scripture for apparent faults: "If in reading Scripture you balk at some thought which though good in itself, yet makes you stumble and fall, blame yourself. Do not despair of finding a spiritual meaning in this stumbling-block; the words: 'Those who believe will not be disappointed' [Rom. 9:33] can be applied to you too. First believe and then beneath the apparent scandal you will find something very useful spiritually." Cited in Jean Daniélou, *Origen*, trans. Walter Mitchell (New York: Sheed and Ward, 1955), p. 182. In *Inferno* 20 and *Purgatorio* 22, Dante could conceivably be writing for a reader like Origen; he could be composing cruxes, errors, and contradictions for someone who hunts for the truth by stumbling over "scandals."

37. The clustering of errors in *Inferno* 20 can be similarly interpreted. When Dante "corrects" Virgil, edits the *Pharsalia*, and condemns the pagan seers, he enters a relation to history that modern historians would fault as anachronistic. If Dante is even dimly aware that he has violated temporal proprieties when he corrects his sources and revises their histories, then one set of errors could conceivably serve as a commentary on the other. Dante synchronizes his miscitations of the great Latin "histories" of the Middle Ages with the classical poet's distressingly modern depiction of Dante's Italy.

38. Many of the characters in Dante's poetry (especially the female characters) have revealing names. In some cases the relation be-

tween name and identity is direct: e.g., Giovanna/Primavera, Pia, and Beatrice. In other cases the punning logic is ironic: e.g., Costanza, Maestro Adamo, and Pier della Vigna. In the case of Manto, the name's significance is clearly ironic. Dante reminds us that Manto's name means "cloak" by stripping her bare and exposing her sexual parts: "E quella che ricuopre le mammelle / che tu non vedi, con le trecce sciolte / e ha di là ogne pilosa pelle / Manto fu" (*Inf.* 20.52–55). Another, more subtle divestment occurs during Dante's description of the springs, lakes, and rivers that Manto passes on her way to Mantua. This elaborate description of flowing water has often been celebrated for its precision and praised as if it were a picture drawn from life. Yet this passage, like the story of Manto, is in fact a citation of the *Aeneid*. In the same section of book 10 in which Manto is named, Virgil explains how the water flows from Lake Benacus (Garda) to Mincio, and from there past Mantua to the sea: "Hinc quoque quingentos in se Mezentius [Ocnus] armat, / quos patre Benaco velatus harundine glauca / Mincius infesta ducebat in aequora pinu (*Aen.* 10. 204–206); "[Ocnus, Manto's son] arms forty men against Mezentius, men whom Mincius, veiled with grey reeds, leads in warships down from father Benacus." The Virgilian passage is considerably briefer than Dante's, but it is, from a rhetorical point of view, far richer. A scene that Dante renders in naturalistic detail is represented by Virgil through a dense network of personifications. Virgil refers to Benacus as "patre Benaco" because that lake is the "father"—source—of the river Mincius. The river is depicted not as a passive waterway upon which Ocnus sails his ships, but as an active agent who, veiled in reeds, leads ("ducebat") the ships of the Latin soldiers down to the sea. Dante's version seems, by comparison, reduced, denuded, and sterilized, a retelling of the same facts with the surface of metaphor stripped away.

39. The translation from the *Convivio* follows *The Banquet*, trans. Christopher Ryan (Saratoga, Calif.: ANMA Libri, 1989). In this passage, *manto* plays the role more typically filled by *velo* or *velame*.

40. Perhaps the most famous instance of a medieval poet toying with interpretive aggression is Chaucer's construction of the Wife of Bath. Whether her comic excesses as a "gloser" are seen as a male author's parody of feminine presumption or as the female character's conscious parody of a male interpretive tradition, her performance clearly invites us to laugh at the distortions that militant, self-interested reading can produce. If "glosynge" were not at least potentially

comic for Chaucer and his audience, it would be very difficult to make sense of the Wife's endless prologue, or, for that matter, the tales of the Nun's Priest, the Manciple, and the Clerk. Jean de Meun, Petrarch, and Boccaccio also play elaborate games in which the medieval enthusiasm for glossing is parodied. One might consider, in this regard, Jean's *Vieille*, Petrarch's letter on climbing Mt. Ventoux, or the entire sequence of patient Griselda stories. On the general development of glossing as a concept and its acquisition of negative connotations in the Middle Ages, see Robert Hanning, "'I Shal Finde It in a Maner Glose': Versions of Textual Harassment in Medieval Literature," in *Medieval Texts and Contemporary Readers*, ed. Laurie Finke and Martin Shichtman (Ithaca, N.Y.: Cornell University Press, 1987), pp. 27–50.

Chapter Four

1. The approach to Dante's science that I am urging in this chapter differs from most previous accounts in the emphasis it places on surprise and play. It does, however, bear other strong affinities and owe other debts to recent studies of Dante's cosmological poetry. The gap between ideal structure and real experience is, for example, a major issue in Patrick Boyde, *Dante: Philomythes and Philosopher* (Cambridge: Cambridge University Press, 1981); Jeffrey Schnapp, *The Transfiguration of History at the Center of Dante's "Paradise"* (Princeton: Princeton University Press, 1986); and Robert Durling and Ronald Martinez, *Time and the Crystal* (Berkeley: University of California Press, 1990).

2. Edward Moore, "The Astronomy of Dante," in *Studies in Dante*, 3d ser. (Oxford: Clarendon Press, 1903), p. 106.

3. The Northern Hemisphere is *discoperta* because it contains land that rises above the level of the ocean. The Southern Hemisphere is, according to Dante, entirely covered with water. See his *Quaestio ad aquam et terram*.

4. The term "sign" should be distinguished here from the term "constellation." Whereas "constellation" signifies a collection of stars, a "sign" is a segment of the ecliptic marked out by the sun in its yearly journey. The sun's position at spring equinox is defined as the first point in Aries, and the rest of the ecliptic is divided into twelve equal segments (signs) beginning at that point. It is thus tautological to state that the sun is entering the *sign* of Aries at spring equinox. The dis-

tinction between signs and constellations is significant because the position of the sun at spring equinox is continually shifting with respect to the sphere of the fixed stars, and hence with respect to the constellations of the zodiac. At spring equinox in 1 A.D., the sun was located in the constellation as well as the sign Aries. Today (or, for that matter, in 1300) the sun is no longer to be found in the *constellation* Aries at spring equinox—it is found instead in the constellation Pisces. Signs, rather than constellations, are given priority in astronomical calculations, and it is the signs of the ecliptic that Dante would have had inscribed on his astrolabe.

5. For more help, see M. A. Orr, *Dante and the Early Astronomers* (London: Wingate, 1913), or Boyde, *Dante: Philomythes*, pp. 144–72.

6. On an astrolabe or star chart the "two motions" appear as intersecting circles; on an armillary sphere they appear as intersecting circular bands (Figures 8 and 9). As one can see from both types of figure, there are two points where the two circles (movements) cross—a point in the sign of Aries and a point in the sign of Libra. It is one of these crossing points—presumably the crossing point in Aries—that is pointed out in *Paradiso* 10.

7. John Freccero, "The Dance of the Stars," in *Dante: The Poetics of Conversion*, ed., Rachel Jacoff (Cambridge, Mass.: Harvard University Press, 1986), p. 240.

8. *Timaeus*, book 1, sec. 36B, trans. Francis Cornford, *Plato's Cosmology* (New York: Humanities Press, 1952), p. 73. In Plato's account, the world soul is apportioned according to the numbers of the Pythagorean Lambda (1, 2, 3, 4, 8, 9, 27). The number 27 is the largest in this sequence, and is also the number of lines included in Dante's invocation in canto 10.

9. Abelard, *Theologia christiana* 2 (*Patrologiae Latina* 178.1172). Cited in Winthrop Wetherbee, *Platonism and Poetry in the Twelfth Century* (Princeton: Princeton University Press, 1972), p. 39. For a history of the association, see Jean Daniélou, *A History of Early Christian Doctrine* (Philadelphia: Westminster Press, 1973), 2: 347.

10. Hugo Rahner, *Greek Myths and Christian Mystery*, trans. B. Battershaw (London: Burns and Oates, 1957), p. 49.

11. Ibid., pp. 89–176.

12. Manfred Porena, "Noterelle dantesche," *Studi Romanzi* 20 (1930): 201–6.

13. See, for example, Boyde, *Dante Philomythes*, p. 240. Before the publication of Porena's article on 29.1–9, this was the accepted reading of the passage.

14. Porena dismisses the eclipse as an accident; Boyde notes the eclipse but seems less interested in it than in the image's broader cosmological significance. My own interest in the eclipse was sparked ten years ago by a note in Dorothy Sayers's and Barbara Reynolds's edition of the *Paradiso*, in which it was suggested that the eclipse represented a planned abstraction. *Paradiso*, trans. Sayers and Reynolds (Harmondsworth, Eng.: Penguin, 1962), p. 313. It should be noted that the eclipse occurs as a result of the very specific set of conditions that Dante imposes. Because the orbits of sun and moon are not strictly coplanar, it is possible for the sun and moon to occupy opposite positions in the zodiac without an eclipse occurring. (If this were not the case, every "full moon" would be eclipsed.) What makes the balancing act an eclipse is Dante's insistence that the planets balance themselves *perfectly*—i.e., are *exactly* opposite one another in the sky and on the horizon.

15. Luke 23:44–66.

16. For a broad structural reading, see my "The Eclipses in the *Paradiso*," *Stanford Italian Review* 9 (1990): 5–32. For a more focused discussion of this particular eclipse and its theological significance, see Alison Cornish, "Planets and Angels in *Paradiso* XXIX: The First Moment," *Dante Studies* 108 (1990): 1–28.

17. It does play a useful role in the experiment, however. By noting explicitly that the distant image is smaller, Dante reminds us that he is *not* discussing the intensity of a point source like a star or a very distant candle. For in the case of point sources (sources whose apparent size does not diminish with distance), observed intensity is, in fact, a function of distance. The more distant a star, the less bright it appears.

18. C. Grandgent, *La Divina Commedia* (Boston: Heath, 1933), p. 20. For the early history of the experiment's reception and the debate over its accuracy, see Alessandro Parronchi, "La perspettiva dantesca," *Studi danteschi* 36 (1958–59): 73–74.

19. The reasons that Dante's experiment has often been misunderstood are neatly summarized in the following passage from James Gibson's *The Perception of the Visual World* (Westport, Conn.: Greenwood Press, 1974), p. 137: "Brightness is sometimes listed as a cue

to distance, the presumable assumption being that an object neces-
sarily appears darker as its distance from the eye increases. . . . [Apart
from atmospheric conditions,] the assumption has no basis in physi-
cal fact. It is true that a point-source of light yields an intensity at the
eye which decreases in proportion to the square of the distance, but
an illuminated surface yields the same intensity *per unit solid angle* at
the eye when it is far as when it is near, and hence possesses the same
brightness under both conditions." It is clear that Dante is *not* mod-
eling his light source as a point source because he claims that the light
source appears smaller in the distant mirror.

20. On the philosophical and scholastic treatments of the ques-
tion, see Paget Toynbee, *Dante Studies and Researches* (London: Me-
thuen, 1902), pp. 78–86, and Bruno Nardi, "La dottrina delle mac-
chie lunari nel secondo canto del *Paradiso*," in *Saggi di filosofia dantes-
ca* (Milan: Società Anonima Editrice Dante Alighieri, 1930). Of the
many discussions of moonspots, Toynbee cites Averroes's *De sub-
stantia Orbis* as among the most relevant; it is cited in Dante's *Quaes-
tio de situ et forma aquae et terrae* and in the *Roman de la rose*. Averroes
claims explicitly that "raritate et densitate" are the "causae illumina-
tionis et obscuritatis" (chap. 2) (the theory Dante champions in the
Convivio and repudiates in *Paradiso* 2). Even more striking is Nature's
long discussion of moonspots in the *Roman de la rose*. After noting that
the word for "universe" in Greek—*aplanos*—means "a thing without
error," Nature admits the following concern: "I do not complain of
the seven planets, each of them is bright, shining, and clean, through-
out the whole of its course. It seems to men that the moon may in-
deed not be clean and pure, because in some places it shows up dark.
. . . What makes its light fail is the fact that the clear part of its sub-
stance cannot reflect the rays that the sun throws out toward it; in-
stead they pass on through and beyond." *Roman de la Rose*, trans. Charles
Dahlberg (Hanover, N.H.: University Press of New England, 1971),
vv. 16833–45. Eventually Nature suggests an "example" that will clarify
her claim—an "example" comparing the moon to a mirror. For a dis-
cussion of Jean de Meun's handling of moonspots, see Earl Jeffrey
Richards, *Dante and the "Roman de la Rose"* (Tübingen: Max Niemey-
er Verlag, 1981), pp. 90–94.

21. *Convivio*, ed. Cesare Vasoli and Domenico De Robertis (Na-
ples: Riccardo Ricciardi, 1988), 2.14.72–6. In fact, it only *presumes*
to lay the hypothesis to rest, because though the mirror experiment

is itself valid, the extrapolation from mirror to moon is flawed. The smooth polished surface of a mirror and the rough surface of the moon reflect light in fundamentally different ways; we do not see an *image* of the sun reflected in the moon as we see an *image* of a lamp reflected in the mirror. If the moon were farther from the earth and, more importantly, farther from the sun, it would appear both smaller *and* less bright.

22. For Roger Bacon's position, see *De multiplicatione specierum: Roger Bacon's Philosophy of Nature*, ed. and trans. David Lindberg (New York: Oxford University Press, 1983), pp. 208–9. See also A. C. Crombie, *Robert Grosseteste and the Origins of Experimental Science, 1100–1700* (Oxford: Clarendon Press, 1953).

23. See, for example, the enthusiasm of the physicist Mark Peterson: "I believe a comment [on the experiment] *is* called for. The comment is, Dante is correct! . . . It's true!" "Dante's Physics," in *The Divine Comedy and the Encyclopedia of Arts and Sciences*, ed. Giuseppe Di Scipio and Aldo Scaglione (Amsterdam: John Benjamins, 1988), p. 170. Nardi speculates that this part of the moonspot lesson might perhaps be adapted from the Italian scientist Pietro d'Abano, who died six years before Dante. "La dottrina," pp. 59–61.

24. I have Rachel Jacoff to thank for pointing out this remarkable fact to me.

25. Moore, *Studies* pp. 88–91.

26. Umberto Bosco and Giovanni Reggio, eds., *La Divina Commedia* (Florence: Le Monnier, 1978), 3: 100; emphasis mine.

27. This point is noted by James Miller in "Three Mirrors of Dante's *Paradiso*," *University of Toronto Quarterly* 46, 3 (Spring 1977): 261–79; Miller does not, however, note the problematic consequences of the extra mirror.

28. For an analogously arch admission of a difficulty, consider *Inf.* 20.97–99: "Però t'assenno che, *se tu mai odi* / originar la mia terra altrimenti, / la verità nulla menzogna frodi." In Hell it is clear that Dante has already heard the "other version," and in Paradise it is clear that he has already performed the experiment (how else could he put it in Beatrice's mouth?).

29. One could argue that such patience is misplaced and that the difficulty of the scientific excursions is thus largely illusory. We should not get too excited if things scientific occasionally go wrong because it is not clear, after all, how much rigor can be expected of a poet's

optics or astronomy. A writer may assume an exacting, didactic pose, but that does not prove that he expects his readers to take that pose too seriously. Even some of the most energetic explicators of Dante's science have, on occasion, voiced this sentiment. When Moore finds himself confronting an apparent astronomical contradiction—the inconsistent presentation of Venus as a *morning* planet in *Purgatorio* 1—he reminds himself (and his readers) of the difference between reality and realism: "To say that a poet must verify the position of Venus at an assumed date before he can put 'the bright and morning star' into his picture would surely be (to borrow an expression of Metastasio) 'confondere il vero col verisimile.'" This is sensible-sounding advice, but we should not be too quick to embrace it. Any decision to wink at a problem is one that needs close inspection: the danger is that while we may think that we are indulging the poet, we may in fact be indulging ourselves. Moore is, I think, guilty of this. He does not deploy terms like "fancy" and "verisimilitude" consistently, but wheels them in only when he cannot quite manage to demonstrate Dante's "power of luminous exposition." The distinction between reality and realism matters only when a thorough scientific analysis of the poem would seem to cast doubt on its author's competence and reliability. The introduction of these concepts thus seems to reflect not methodological sophistication but merely frustration.

30. This point is made rather elegantly in Sinclair's note on canto 13. *The Divine Comedy: Paradiso*, with translation and commentary by John D. Sinclair (Oxford: Oxford University Press, 1939), p. 197.

31. See Douglas Biow, "From Ignorance to Knowledge: The Marvelous in *Inferno* 13," in *The Poetry of Allusion: Virgil and Ovid in Dante's Commedia*, ed. Rachel Jacoff and Jeffrey Schnapp (Stanford: Stanford University Press, 1991), p. 61.

32. See John Freccero, "Introduction to the *Paradiso*," in *Poetics of Conversion*, ed. Jacoff, pp. 209–20, or Marguerite Chiarenza, "The Imageless Vision and Dante's *Paradiso*," *Dante Studies* 90 (1972): 77–91.

33. It is nice to see that one of the sights that Dante notices in his backward glance is the moon divested of its shadows: "Vidi la figlia di Latona incensa / sanza quell'ombra che mi fu cagione / per che già la credetti rara e densa" (*Par.* 22.139–41).

34. Rachel Jacoff, "The Post-Palinodic Smile: *Paradiso* VIII and IX," *Dante Studies* 98 (1980): 111–22.

35. See also Giuseppe Mazzotta, "*Theologia Ludens*: Angels and Devils in the *Divine Comedy*," in *Discourses of Authority*, in *Medieval and Renaissance Literature*, ed. Kevin Brownlee and Walter Stevens (Hanover, N.H.: University Press of New England, 1987), pp. 216–35.

36. "Lo ministro maggior della natura / che del valor del ciel lo mondo imprenta / e col suo lume il tempo ne misura, / con quella parte che sù si rammenta / congiunto, si girava." (*Par*. 10.28–32).

37. Thomas Aquinas, *Summa Theologica*, tertia, qu. 24.

38. For the astronomical treatises, see Lynn Thorndike, *The Sphere of Sacrobosco and Its Commentators* (Chicago: University of Chicago Press, 1949). For Sacrobosco's observations, see pp. 116–17; for Michael Scot's, see p. 341; and for Cecco D'Ascoli's, see p. 411.

39. *Hymnarius paraclitensis*, cited in Rahner, *Greek Myths*, p. 117.

40. For examples, see Paul Thorby, *Le Crucifix* (Nantes: Bellanger, 1959), or J. E. Hunt, *English and Welsh Crucifixes 670–1550* (London: S.P.C.K., 1957). To overcome the obvious problem of representing an eclipsed (i.e., invisible) sun and moon, artists were obliged to employ a variety of visual metaphors. One method is to depict both the sun and the moon as thin crescents (plates 27 and 29 in *Le Crucifix*). Another method is to veil the sun and the moon behind clouds or behind the garments of an angel (plates 208–11 in *Le Crucifix*). In an exceptionally emphatic display of the eclipse, a personified sun and moon hide their own faces in veils (plate 29 in *Le Crucifix* and p. 27 in *English and Welsh Crucifixes*).

41. "E come donna onesta che permane / di sé sicura, e per l'altrui fallanza, / pur ascoltando, timida si fane, / così Beatrice trasmutò sembianza; / e tale eclissi credo che 'n ciel fue / quando patì la suprema possanza" (*Par*. 27.31–36).

42. Jeffrey Schnapp, "Unica Spes Hominum, Crux, O Venerabile Signum," in Schnapp, *Transfiguration*, pp. 70–169.

43. *Timaeus*, trans. Cornford, p. 31.

44. The significance of cosmological vagaries is discussed in the final chapter of *Time and the Crystal*. Durling and Martinez there suggest that Dante's attention to "variances between convention and reality" may have dark implications for his astrologically ratified prophecies; these variances, they speculate, may reflect Dante's awareness of the fine distinction between truth and counterfeit (p.

255). Schnapp discusses Dante's harmonization of both cosmic and historical violence in his chapter on the cross in his *Transfiguration* (pp. 70–169).

45. "Virtù diversa fa diversa lega / col prezioso corpo ch'ella avviva / nel qual, sì come vita in voi, si lega" (Diverse virtues make diverse alloy with the precious body it quickens, wherein, even as life in you, it is bound; *Par.* 2.139–41).

Chapter 5

1. See Paul Frankel, *The Gothic: Literary Sources and Interpretations Through Eight Centuries* (Princeton: Princeton University Press, 1960). Vasari describes the creations of "Gothic" architects variously as "mostruosi" and "barbari" and claims that they are without order: "Che più tosto confusione o disordine si può chiamare" (cited in Frankel, p. 860). Rabelais's Gargantua is no less harsh in his assessment of Gothic literature: "Les temps éstoit encore tenebreux et setant l'infelicite et la calamite des Gothz, qui avoient mis a destruction toute bonne literature" (cited in Frankel, p. 859). The French critic Roland Fréart de Chambray (1707) has these words of dispraise: "The Universal and unreasonable Thickness of the Walls, Clumsy Buttresses, Towers, sharp pointed Arches, Doors and other Apertures, without proportion; Non-sense Insertions of various Marbles impertinently plac'd; Turrets, and Pinacles thick set with *Munkies* and *Chimeares* (and abundance of busy Work and other Incongruities) dissipate, and break the Angels of the Sight, and so Confound it, that one cannot consider it with any Steadiness, where to begin or end" (cited in Frankel, p. 863).

2. For Male's attempts to marginalize the monster's role in Gothic art, see *The Gothic Image*, trans. Dora Nussey (New York: Icon Editions, 1972), pp. 58–63.

3. The name "Geryon" clearly derives from Latin sources, but the classical Geryon who is slain by Hercules is a substantially different type of monster: according to *Aeneid* 8.202, Geryon is a monster with three bodies and three heads. Dante's more complex monster has been seen variously to resemble the beasts of Apocalypse 9 and the Indian Mantichora—a creature with the face of a man and the stinging tail of a scorpion. Geryon seems not to be derived from a single text, but to be a pastiche of classical, biblical, and encyclopedic sources.

4. On the role of error in romance narratives, see Patricia Parker, *Inescapable Romance: Studies in the Poetics of a Mode* (Princeton: Princeton University Press, 1979), pp. 16–53.

5. See John Freccero's essays, "Pilgrim in a Gyre," "Dante's Ulysses: From Epic to Novel," and "Infernal Inversion and Christian Conversion: *Inferno* XXXIV," in *Dante: The Poetics of Conversion*, ed. Rachel Jacoff (Cambridge, Mass.: Harvard University Press, 1986).

6. For a discussion of Dante's narrative technique in the Malebolge, see Teodolinda Barolini's "Narrative and Style in Lower Hell," *Annali d'Italianistica* 8 (1990): 314–44.

7. Franco Ferrucci notes the centrality of the encounter in his essay, "The Meeting with Geryon," in Ferrucci, *The Poetics of Disguise: The Autobiography of the Work in Homer, Dante, and Shakespeare*, trans. Ann Dunnigan (Ithaca, N.Y.: Cornell University Press, 1980), pp. 66–102. Though Ferrucci is not especially concerned with structural questions, my reading of Geryon is much informed by his essay.

8. C. Grandgent, *La Divina Commedia* (Boston: Heath, 1933), p. xxxiv.

9. *Apologia ad Guillelmum*, *Patrologiae Latina* 182, cols. 914–16. Translation is from G. G. Coulton *Life in the Middle Ages*, 2d ed. (Cambridge: Cambridge University Press,1930), 4:169–74. See also Umberto Eco, *The Aesthetics of Thomas Aquinas* (Cambridge, Mass.: Harvard University Press, 1988), pp. 6–10.

10. *City of God* 26.8.

11. Horace also uses a monster as a figure for artistic error at the very start of his *Epistula ad Pisones* (the *Ars poetica*). Horace's "ridiculous" monster symbolizes a monstrous mixture of genres: "If a painter chose to join a human head to the neck of a horse, and to spread the feathers of many a hue over the limbs picked up now here now there, so that what at the top is a lovely woman ends below in a black and ugly fish, could you, my friends, if favored with a private view refrain from laughing? Believe me, dear Pisos, quite like such pictures would be a book, whose idle fancies shall be shaped like a sick man's dreams, so that neither head nor foot can be assigned to a single shape."

12. Already in the wood of the suicide, for example, Dante hints that his fiction is "incredible." But with Geryon's emergence into the poem, such implicit fears actually come to the surface; for the first time in the *Inferno*, Dante expressly pleads for his readers' faith. The oath has been subject to several contradictory readings. In his "Meet-

ing with Geryon," Ferrucci argues for an essentially ironic reading; Hollander and Barolini have argued instead for the oath's importance as a guide to the *Comedy*'s genre. See Hollander, "Dante *Theologus-Poeta*," in *Studies in Dante*, (Ravenna: Longo, 1980), p. 76, and Barolini, *Dante's Poets: Textuality and Truth in the Comedy* (Princeton: Princeton University Press, 1984), pp. 213–14.

13. *Convivio*, ed. Cesare Vasoli and Domenico De Robertis (Naples: Riccardo Ricciardi, 1988), 2.1.3. The translation from the *Convivio* follows *The Banquet*, trans. Christopher Ryan (Saratoga, Calif.: ANMA Libri, 1989).

14. Albert Ascoli, *Ariosto's Bitter Harmony* (Princeton: Princeton University Press, 1987), p. 252. As Ascoli and Freccero note, Ulysses also travels in a spiral.

15. "Ecco la fiera con la coda aguzza" (*Inf.* 17.1). I have Jeffrey Schnapp to thank for pointing this pun out to me.

16. There are two very prominent passages where Chaucer uses Ovid to comment on his own art. The more explicit is the *Prologue to the Man of Law's Tale*. In that prologue, the Man of Law identifies Chaucer as a translator of Ovid, a translator who has worked so industriously that he has left the speaker without any tale to tell. He worries openly and comically that in order to perform for his fellow travelers, he must risk seeming like one of the Pierides. *The Manciple's Tale* involves a subtler but even more telling use of Ovid. The raven, who in *Metamorphoses* 2 represents the gossiping poet, reappears transformed into a crow who can "countrefete the speche of every man." This crow serves as a figure for Chaucer and his art of imitating voices, and the bird's punishment at the hands of Apollo thus serves as an ironic preparation for the retraction. Though the crow, like Chaucer, is guilty of speaking too freely, he is not granted a chance to repent. Indeed, the very moral of *The Manciple's Tale* is the impossibility of achieving an effective retraction: "Thyng that is seyd is seyd, and forth it gooth, / Though hym repente, or be hym nevere so looth." David Hult has explored Guillaume de Lorris's use of the Narcissus myth in similarly self-reflexive terms in *Self-fulfilling Prophecies: Readership and Authority in the First "Roman de la Rose"* (Cambridge: Cambridge University Press, 1986), pp. 291–300.

17. Dante's use of Ovid has been the subject of much recent work. See, for example, *Dante and Ovid: Essays in Intertextuality*, ed. Madison Sowell (Binghamton, N.Y.: MRTS, 1991), and essays on Ovid

in *The Poetry of Allusion: Virgil and Ovid in Dante's Commedia*, ed. Rachel Jacoff and Jeffrey Schnapp (Stanford: Stanford University Press, 1991). The essays in the latter collection by Pamela Macfie, Kevin Brownlee, and Jeffrey Schnapp all touch upon figures mentioned in this chapter—Arachne, Phaeton, and Marsyas.

18. Ovid's story has intriguing resonances with the representation of magpies in the Latin Bestiary tradition. In a twelfth-century Bestiary preserved in the Cambridge University Library, one finds the following entry for "magpie": "The word 'picae' stands for 'poeticae' because they can imitate words in a distinct voice like a man." T. H. White, *The Book of Beasts* (New York: Dover Publications, 1984), p. 138.

19. This interpretation of the invocations is admittedly idiosyncratic. In the eyes of most Dante scholars, emphasis should not be placed on Dante's identification with the Ovidian artist, but on the distinction between them. Singleton translates *seguitando* as "accompanying" and stresses the modesty of Dante's posture: Dante is asking humbly for help from Calliope just as he later binds himself with a "humble" reed (note the pun on "reed"—plant and instrument). According to Singleton, Dante is asking Apollo to help him to "sing as sweetly as the god played when he vanquished the satyr." (In fact, there is no mention of Apollo's singing in the invocation, and Dante refers only to the god's flaying of the unfortunate satyr; it is the threat of punishment, not the hope of assistance, that Dante emphasizes here and that Ovid emphasizes in the *Metamorphoses*.) For a more recent treatment of *Paradiso* 1 that takes fuller account of the invocation's complexity but still stresses Dante's piety, see Kevin Brownlee's "Pauline Vision and Ovidian Speech in *Paradiso* 1," in *Poetry of Allusion*, ed. Jacoff and Schnapp. According to Brownlee, Dante effectively "reverses Marsyas's prideful challenge and artistic presumption" (p. 209).

20. See Robert Durling, *The Figure of the Poet in Renaissance Epic* (Cambridge, Mass.: Harvard University Press, 1965), pp. 117–18.

21. See William Anderson's comments on this passage in *Ovid's Metamorphoses—Books 6–10* (Norman: University of Oklahoma Press, 1972). Compared with Athena's rigid, symmetrical weaving, Arachne's seems slightly out of control; its images spill into one another, just as the narrative of the *Metamorphoses* sweeps onward without any clear organizing principle.

22. Karl Galinsky, *Ovid's Metamorphoses* (Berkeley: University of California Press, 1975), p. 51.

23. Each worker has his own phallic tool, but they are not of equal worth: the poet flies like a god while the day-laborers tend to the earth.

24. The two competing alternatives are nicely reflected in two different readings of *Inferno* 24–25. In "Problematical Virtuosity: Dante's Depiction of the Thieves," *Dante Studies* 91 (1973): 27–45, Richard Terdiman casts Dante as an essentially Ovidian poet. In "Virtuosity and Virtue: Poetic Self-Reflection in the *Commedia*," *Dante Studies* 98 (1980): 1–18, Peter Hawkins responds that Dante stages the Ovidian error in order to repudiate it.

Epilogue

1. *Il mistero dell' amor platonico* (London: Taylor, 1850). Concerning this work, Rossetti's biographer, E. R. Vincent, has the following words: "It is to be hoped that those who are tempted to be his disciples may first inform themselves of the unscientific and purely casual way in which this fantastic theory grew in its author's brain, and perhaps, too, be warned by this example of a pitiful waste of remarkable powers of application and imagination." *Gabriele Rossetti in England* (Oxford: Clarendon Press, 1936), p. 110.

2. See Vincent, *Rossetti in England*, p. 37.

3. Edward Allen Fay, *Concordance of the Divina Commedia* (Boston: Little, Brown, 1888). A professor in the National Deaf-Mute College in Kendal Green, Washington, D.C., Fay completed his arduous, 800-page project in the "leisure hours" of a four-year period. Fay admits the "drudgery" of his task, but claims that his "constantly increasing familiarity with the *sacrato poema*" more than compensates and even compares himself to Dante picking flowers in Earthly Paradise. Agnelli also has recourse to the imagery of bucolic asylum: "Entrato come insegnante in un instituto di sordo-muti, l'illustrazione del viaggio dantesco, lungamente vagheggiata, mi si ripresentò come mezzo propizio a riempire l'intervalli non destinati all'istruzione, ed a trasportarmi, se mi si permette la manzoniana espressione, *in più spirabil aere*." Giovanni Agnelli, *Topo-cronografia del viaggio dantesco* (Milan: Hoepli, 1891), p. 5 (emphasis in original).

Index of Passages Cited from Dante

Index

In this index a continuous discussion over two or more pages is indicated by a span of page numbers, e.g., "57–59." *Passim* is used for a cluster of references in close but not consecutive sequence.

Library of Congress Cataloging-in-Publication Data

Kleiner, John.
    Mismapping the underworld : daring and error in Dante's Comedy /
John Kleiner.
        p.   cm. — (Figurae)
    Includes bibliographical references and index.
    ISBN 0-8047-2143-2
    1. Dante Alighieri, 1265–1321. Divina commedia.   2. Errors and
blunders, Literary.   I. Title.   II. Series: Figurae (Stanford,
Calif.)
PQ4374.K54   1994
851'.1—dc20   93-19358
                                                                CIP

⊗ This book is printed on acid-free paper.